WITHDRAWN

THE BOLLINGEN SERIES XXIV

ANDRÉ MALRAUX

THE PSYCHOLOGY OF ART

THE TWILIGHT
OF THE ABSOLUTE

TRANSLATED BY
STUART GILBERT

THE BOLLINGEN SERIES XXIV

PANTHEON BOOKS

CONTENTS

ILLUSTRATIONS

ETRUSCAN ART. MASTARNA (CA. 380 B. C.)

THE TWILIGHT OF THE ABSOLUTE

Though, in respect of art, we are the first to be heirs of all the earth, our heritage has undergone the most elaborate metamorphosis that the world has ever known.

German archaeologists have told us repeatedly that our idea of Greece is a pure convention, and though their insistence often seemed excessive, we must own that they

"MASTER OF THE REEDS." (GREECE, Vth CENT. B. C.)

were in the right. Their mistake lay in setting up against a convention, a reconstitution. For, though our art museums conjure up for us a Greece that never was, the Greek works of art in them patently exist; Athens was never white, but her statues, now bereft of colour, have conditioned the sensibility of Europe. And the elaborate reconstitutions Munich has shown us have failed to replace, by what Greek sculptors probably intended, what the statues certainly convey to us to-day. Whatever view we take of ancient Greek statuary, the present state of things is the result not of a convention but of a metamorphosis.

A metamorphosis affecting all ancient art. The Germans sought to bring Greece back to life, alleging that her works of art reached our museums in the state of corpses. Singularly fertile "corpses," in that case; nor did the gallery of waxworks set up in their stead have any such fertility. The argument, of course, is that "we ought to see these works as those for whom they were created saw them."

But what, if any, bygone work can be seen in that manner?

If the impression made on us to-day by a painted and waxed Greek head is not that of a work of art recalled to life, but that of a grotesque, the reason is not simply that we are dupes of a convention; it is also because this one resuscitated style emerges among a host of styles that are not thus resuscitated. Which brings home the vastness of the metamorphosis; in the East almost all statues were painted: those of Central Asia, India, China and Japan. Roman statuary was often in all the colours different marbles could provide. Romanesque statues were painted, so were most Gothic statues (notably those in wood). There is evidence that pre-Columbian idols were painted, as were the Mayan bas-reliefs. Yet the whole past has reached us . . . colourless.

Also it has reached us (until the Christian era) without its painting. Greek painting in the age of Pericles was doubtless two-dimensional, and perhaps the elements in common between the white lecythi and the Naples *Knuckle-bones Players* give us some notion of its style. As for hoping to discover what it was by a study of Pompeian decorative art, we might as well believe that in the year 4000, it will be possible to understand the art of to-day by studying our posters. Those Greek artists whose grapes, we are told, were so realistic that even the birds were taken in, were contemporaries of Alexander, not of Themistocles. The chief paintings associated with

ALEXANDER THE ATHENIAN (FIRST CENT. B. C.).   THE KNUCKLE-BONES PLAYERS (FRAGMENT)

Buddhism that Asia has bequeathed to us were made long after Buddha's day. Moreover, the painting on the walls of the Ajanta caves and on Romanesque statues has come to us transformed, sometimes by the mere lapse of time, sometimes by decay, and the transformation wrought by these is not one of degree but of kind. Our taste, not to mention our aesthetic, is no less responsive to this subtle attenuation of colours, once bright to the point of garishness, than that of the last century was to the thick coat of varnish on the pictures in museums. If for us an intact Romanesque Virgin (Italy has several such) and a time-worn Virgin of Auvergne clearly pertain to the same art, this is not because the Auvergne Virgin is a mutilated replica of the other, but because the intact Virgin shares, *in a less degree,* the characteristics we discern in the time-worn Virgin. Romanesque art, as we know it, is an art of stone-carving : of bas-reliefs and pier-statues. Our museums house wooden figures akin to the bas-reliefs, reft from their setting and usually in a damaged state. And when it chances to be intact, a Romanesque *Descent from the Cross* seems often to reduce the majesty of "true" Romanesque to the art of the Breton wayside crosses or the Christchild's crib. Indeed we are no more anxious to restore to the great Romanesque crucifix in the Louvre its pedestal than her missing arms to the Venus of Melos ; of the two versions of Romanesque, we have chosen ours.

Every resuscitation sorts out what it recalls to life. We see this filtering process at work in the early collections of ancient works, despite restorations. Our museums

ROMANESQUE ITALIAN ART. DESCENT FROM THE CROSS

welcome torsos but not limbs. That fortunate mutilation which contributes to the glory of the Venus of Melos might be the work of some inspired antiquary; for mutilations, too, have a style. And the choice of the fragments that are preserved is far from being haphazard; we do not hesitate to prefer Lagash statues without their heads, Khmer Buddhas without their bodies, and Assyrian wild animals isolated from their contexts. Accidents impair and Time transforms, but it is we who choose.

From the seventeenth to the nineteenth century pictures, "translated" by engraving, became prints; they kept their drawing and lost their colours, which were replaced (through a process of interpretation, not copying) by an "expression" of their colours in black-and-white. They also lost their dimensions, and acquired margins. It is common knowledge that during the nineteenth century the successive layers of varnish put on pictures were by way of creating a "museum style," involving a preposterous kinship between Titian and Tintoretto — pending the day cleaning was to put a stop to this absurd fraternity.

Neither Titian nor Tintoretto had asked posterity to overlay his canvases with a yellow gloss; and if the ancient statues have gone white, Pheidias is not to blame, nor is Canova. Yet it was only after painting had become bright that the overlay of varnish came to seem intolerable to the curators of our museums.

A period that does not filter an art of the past makes no effort to resuscitate it in its original form; but merely ignores it. That in the Middle Ages the white statues, though they were there to see, were never looked at, is doubtless due to the fact that theirs was a dead style; but it is also a fact that certain cultures have banned metamorphosis as passionately as ours has welcomed it.

It was not because of any taste for the past that Christian art admitted reminiscences of Pompeii in some of its miniatures of the High Middle Ages. The notion of art as such must first have come into being, if the past is to acquire its value; thus for a Christian to see a classical statue as a statue, and not as a heathen idol, or a mere puppet, he would have needed to begin by seeing in a "Virgin" a statue, before seeing it as the Virgin.

What religion appreciates the idols of another religion? If the effigies of the old gods escaped destruction, they owed this to their prestige of "antiquity." It is only when the concept of art arises — when the "heathen" god has become a statue — that they are safe from iconoclasts. But the past had another enemy, and this was a highly cultured one: the notion of the absolute superiority of contemporary art. The Church, which, up to the eighteenth century, championed "modern" art, allowed the Gothic frescos to be whitewashed, and humanist Popes were much readier to collect antiques than to protect Romanesque churches. A culture which wishes to defend not only the forms of art in which its own is included, but also the most it can of the art of the past, owns to, or implies, the view that there are more things on earth (and under it) than are dreamt of in its own philosophy.

It does not demur at bringing together arts that in appearance are utterly different. But this union is rendered feasible only by the metamorphosis that the works of the past have undergone, not merely through the ravages of time but also because they are, in some measure, detached from a part of that which they once expressed. For, could we bring ourselves to feel what the first spectators of an Egyptian statue, or a Romanesque crucifixion, felt, we would make haste to transfer them from our museums to sanctuaries befitting them. True, we are trying more and more to gauge the feelings of those "first spectators," but without forgetting our own, and we can be contented all the more easily with a mere knowledge of these, devoid of actual experience, because there is far less question of putting the work of art to its service than of putting this knowledge to the service of the work of art.

It is possible that the deepest feelings of a culture disappear when it passes away ; that an Egyptian's feeling for the sacrosanct must for ever remain unknown to us. Nevertheless, such feelings, when expressed in works of art, are not without effect on us ; thus, though we have only the vaguest notions of what a Hebrew prophet was really like, the Old Testament has none the less bulked large in the evolution of the idea of justice throughout the world. But the work of art that speaks to us as such is a very real presence ; in a world in which even the name of Christ had been forgotten, a Chartres statue would still be a statue. And if, in that civilization, the idea of art had survived, the statue still would speak a language. What language? it may be asked. But what language is spoken by those pre-Columbians of whom we still know next to nothing, or by the coins of ancient Gaul, or by those bronzes of the Steppes as to which we do not even know what were the peoples who cast them? What language is spoken by the bisons of the caves?

Every surviving work of art becomes a fragment. Often it is one, literally. Always deprived of something, if only of the setting of its age. Thus long ago a work of sculpture lorded it in a temple, a street, or a reception-room. All of these now are lost to it. Even if the reception-room is "reconstructed" in a museum, even if the statue has kept its place in the portal of its cathedral, the town which surrounded the reception-room or the cathedral has changed. There is no getting round the banal truth that for thirteenth-century man Gothic art was "modern," and the Gothic world a present reality, not a phase of history. If we replace faith by love of art, little does it matter if a cathedral chapel is reconstituted faithfully, stone by stone, in a museum ; for we have begun by converting our cathedrals into museums. Metamorphosis is no accident, but a law of its being, for every work of art.

That (to quote a famous definition) a religious picture "before being a Virgin, is a flat surface covered with colours arranged in a certain order" is true for us, but anyone who had spoken thus to the men who made the statuary of Saint Denis would have been laughed out of court. For them, as for Suger, and also for Saint Bernard, what was being made was a Virgin ; and only, in a very secondary sense, an arrangement of colours. The colours were arranged in a certain order not so as to be a statue but so as to be a Virgin. Not to represent a lady having Our Lady's attributes, but to *be* ; to win a place in that other-world of holiness which alone sponsored its quality.

Since these colours "in a certain order" do not merely serve purposes of representation, what purpose do they serve? That of their own order, the modernist replies. An order variable, to say the least : since it is a style. No more than Suger would Michelangelo have admitted that word "before" in "before being a Virgin. . ." He would have said : "Lines and colours must be arranged in a certain order so that a painted Virgin may be worthy of Our Lady." For him, as for Van Eyck, plastic art was, amongst other things, a means of access to a world of the divine. But that world was not separable from their painting, as the model is from the portrait ; it took form through the expression they conferred on it.

Though a Gothic Crucifixion may become a museum statue *qua* work of art, those special relations between its lines and masses which make it a work of art are the creative expression of an emotion far exceeding a mere will to art. It is not of the same family as a crucifixion painted to-day by a talented atheist — out only to express his talent. It is an object, a picture or a work of sculpture, but it is also a Crucifixion. A Gothic head that we admire does not affect us merely through the ordering of its planes ; we discern in it, across the centuries, a gleam of the face of the Gothic Christ. Because that gleam *is there*. . .

The close relationship between painting and poetry is even less understood than that between painting and religion. Yet not only was poetry, throughout the world and for many centuries, one of the elements of art, but over a long period painting was poetry's most favoured mode of expression. Between the death of Dante and the birth of Shakespeare, how trivial seem the poets of Christendom, as compared with Piero della Francesca, Fra Angelico, Botticelli, Piero di Cosimo, Leonardo, Titian and Michelangelo ! What poems contemporary with Watteau rank beside his art?

The distinction drawn to-day between the specific procedures of painting and those of poetry is as artificial as the distinction between form and content. They once comprised an indivisible domain. It was by way of poetry that Leonardo's colours were arranged in a certain order. "*Painting,*" he wrote, "*is a form of poetry made to be seen.*" Until Delacroix, the very notion of great painting was wrapped up with it. Can we suppose it was due to some mere aberration that Duccio, Giotto, Fouquet,

PIERO DI COSIMO. THE DEATH OF PROCRIS

Grünewald, the masters of the Italian Renaissance, Velázquez, Rembrandt, Vermeer, Poussin — not to mention the artists of Asia — shared this view?

When our contemporaries wish to ban poetry from painting, what is it they really wish to ban? Painting with "subjects," like that of the nineteenth century — in other words realistic treatment of the imaginary, the subservience of painting to romantic or moving scenes, often tied up with history. I have already said that, though the modern eye balks at Meissonier's *1814*, with Napoleon on the muddy road, it accepts Rouault's *Vieux Roi*. If the subjects of 1850 art are meretricious, this is because, far from being called into being by the art of those who painted them, they are models to which this art was called on to submit. Titian did not reproduce imagined scenes; it was from the nightbound forests of Cadore he got his "Venus."

Far from excluding poetry from painting, we should do better to realize that all great works of plastic art are steeped in poetry. We can see this no less in Braque's still lifes than in Chagall's fantasies. When a realist has genius poetry comes to him, unsummoned. How can we fail to observe the poetic element in the art of Vermeer, Chardin, even in Breughel, and in Courbet's major works?

We profess to admire only their colour in Hieronymus Bosch and Titian; but if we wished to treat their colour, which served them as the medium for their poetry, as separable from it, we should need to assume that their art was a technique of representation. Realistic as it may often seem, it unites the *Juggler* with the *Temptations*; the trees in Titian's finest works belong *also* to that magic realm of poesy. And this poetic "glamour" is not something superadded to his painting; it is still less separable from it than is the fantastic from the art of Bosch. Nor is it due to the taste prevailing then in Venice, as is the calligraphy of his decorative compositions; it is due solely to his art. This is becoming clearer with the advance in colour reproduction and the greater comprehensiveness of modern exhibitions thanks to loans of masterpieces; far more

BOTTICELLI.   LA DERELITTA

than the drawing, the colour sponsored the poetry in his art. Whereas, when reproduced in black-and-white, Titian, one of the world's greatest poets, seems often no more than a master of tapestry design. True, some of our painters tell us that they would prefer a Titian with Venus left out — meaning that they would rather have those still lifes in which Venus, though no less present than in the Prado, is not recognizable as such. As though *Laura di Dianti, Venus and Adonis,* the Vienna *Callisto,* indeed *The Nymph and the Shepherd,* belonged to the world of Cézanne, or even that of Renoir! Is what differentiates Rembrandt's from almost all Hals's portraits only the difference between two palettes? Or, we might even add, that which differentiates the *"Regents"* from the *Archers?*

With poetry, in this sense, painting has always, to say the least of it, collaborated; and the art of the age of religion collaborated no less than does our modern art. But from the Renaissance up to Delacroix there was more than mere collaboration; poetry was wedded to painting as it once had been to Faith. Leonardo, Rembrandt and Goya seek and achieve both poetic and plastic expression, often simultaneously. Pisanello's hanged men, the daylit vistas of Leonardo, Bosch's nightbound recessions, Rembrandt's light, and Goya's phantoms belong to both categories. The Queen of Sheba is conjured

GOYA. PURE MADNESS

REMBRANDT. THE PRODIGAL SON

LEONARDO DA VINCI. VIRGIN, CHILD AND ST ANNE (ST ANNE)

up by Piero's art, the Prodigal Son by Rembrandt's, Cythera by Watteau's, a limbo of spectres by Goya's. Poetry comes as naturally to this art as its flowers to a plant.

Italian Mannerism affected Europe rather as a school of poetry than through its form; Jean Cousin and Jan Matzys were votaries of a dream and of a dream alone. It is absurd to see mere imitators of forms that they admired, in men who so often invented their own harmonies and whose whole attitude of mind (which soon became a "taste," almost a period *décor*) was so very different from that of their masters. Whom were Primaticcio, Rosso, or Nicola dell'Abbate imitating in their ectoplasm-like convolutions and their mauve Christs? Or Michelangelo, for whom the whole body was a network of sinews, or the Raphael of the Vatican, or he of the Farnesina? Was Cellini another Giulio Romano? No doubt Mannerism owed something to the taste of its period, as Venice and Florence had owed much to the taste of theirs. And, in fact, the Mannerist artists often seem like illustrators; but not in the sense given to that term in the nineteenth century, when literature reigned supreme and illustration was its handmaid. The Mannerists were not out to serve writers but legends — what they called "the fable." And, whatever may be said, their interpretation was not of the same nature as that of the Golden Legend by the mediaevals, who firmly believed in the truth of the tales contained in it; whereas the Mannerists frankly indulged in make-believe on the grand scale, in the service of poetry (not of poets) — and half Europe was conquered by their art.

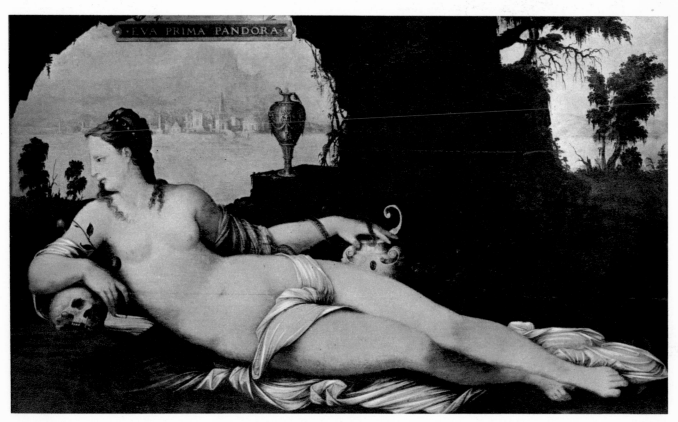

JEAN COUSIN. EVA PRIMA PANDORA

These various "Schools of Fontainebleau" aimed less at the portrayal of a poetic world than at a poetic expression of the visible world. Is there less poetry in *The Harvesters* at the Louvre, or the *Descent into the Cellar* than in *Eva Prima Pandora*, in Caron's pictures, and the countless "Dianas"? The methods of expression we find in the best works of these painters are not invariably "literary": elongation, forms half glimpsed through veils, arabesques often converging on a focal point and more akin to those of glyptics than to those of Alexandria, are definitely pictorial methods, unconcerned with literature.

The importance of Mannerist art in this context is that it illustrates the way in which these methods were conditioned by a poetic impulse, now approaching ours, and now remote from it, turn by turn; it is the element of mystery infusing them which most appeals to us.

JEAN GOURMONT. DESCENT INTO THE CELLAR (1537)

That some of these bygone pictures are imbued with a truly modern poetic emotion — that Piero di Cosimo is very near akin to Chirico — is plain to see. We have even found unfinished etchings by Rembrandt in which his poetic sense comes very near ours ; but let us make no mistake regarding this. Our modern taste has become adjusted to a, so to speak, sectarian poetry which adjusts its world to perspectives of

REMBRANDT. THE PAINTER AND HIS MODEL

the irrational and dream fantasies. And doubtless all true poetry is irrational in the sense that, for the established order of the relations between things, it substitutes a new system of relations. But that new system, long before peopling a void within, was a means of access to a realm of dazzling revelations, a panic conquest of the joys and wonders of the earth ; or that, not of a world of dreams, but of the star-strewn darkness which broods over the august presence of the Mothers or the slumber of the gods. Mallarmé is not a greater poet than Homer, Piero di Cosimo than Titian; and what do the vividest realizations of our painters amount to if we compare their impact with what that first great vision of a nude woman — her of the Panathenaea, on whom the first butterfly alighted — must have meant to those who saw her then, or that of the first sculptured face in which a Christian *recognized* the face of Christ? As between the poetry of the dream and that of exaltation, it is not always the former that creative art has sponsored; Baudelaire's vision of the night ensues on that of Michelangelo, it does not efface it.

It was this sublime poetry that came to take the place, in art, of Faith. Religion and, thereafter, piety ceased to suffice for art, and poetic inspiration tended to exalt the human element, once kept in the background. True, Titian and Rembrandt were believers. But, whereas a great mediaeval crucifixion was a communion and a vener-ation, the *Three Crosses* are, rather, a dialogue of impassioned power, yet none the less a dialogue, and bearing a signature which has become more than a mere trade-mark. For midway between the world of men and the transcendent world of God another world was coming into being, and art was at its service.

Seeking to ascertain to what deep craving of our being a work of art responds is not mere labour lost; and we do well to realize that this craving is not always the same. Throughout the ancient East sculptors made images of the gods, but not haphazard; the artists built up styles which they proceeded to impose on these images, and then devised successive transformations of these styles. Statuary served for the making of gods, and Eastern art served to express, and doubtless to enrich, a special relationship between man and the divine. In Greece also the sculptors made gods; but the artists wrested these gods from *terror antiquus,* from death, from the realm of the non-human. The theocratic spirit of the East had imparted even to profane objects the style they had invented for their sacred figures, indeed the Egyptian perfume-spoons look as if they had been carved for dead women; whereas, with its Hermes and Amphitrite, Greece succeeded in imposing idealized men's forms on the gods. Thus, while in both cases art depicted gods, it is obvious that, in doing this, it directed its appeal to different elements of the human soul.

Though the purpose of all Christian art was to edify, the change in the function of art between Chartres and the completion of St Peter's, between Giotto and Bernini, was as great as that between Egypt and Greece. Gothic art was all a will to truth, an incarnation; Baroque art was all promises, hypotheses, theatrical and pontifical parade. Although, in this case, the religion did not change its name, the basic feelings to which

MICHELANGELO.   NIGHT (FRAGMENT)

art was a response had undergone a vital change. Emancipating the world from all that in it is ephemeral, Giotto painted that which is more real than reality; Jesuit painting set out to charm (as a first step to convincing) with its intimations of what might be, or was some day to be. Christian as it is, this painting has to our mind less in common with great Christian sculpture than with pagan Alexandrian sculpture (which in fact its artists much admired).

Though aware of this, we are apt to forget, when discussing Greek statues and Egyptian statues, *qua* works of sculpture, and likewise Giotto's and Guido's pictures, *qua* works of graphic art, that we are acting as if these works formed part of one and the same domain. But those who made them put art to the service of the works themselves; whereas we subordinate them to art. We take it for granted that the painter's function is to serve painting; indeed if it were genuinely held that his function is to serve (for instance) politics, or to act directly on the spectator like the propagandist or advertiser, the art museum might well die out in under a century. The art museum came into being when the view became generally accepted that the artist's initial stimulus was a wish to make what we call a picture. And here we have a metamorphosis, subtle but sweeping — and all the more so for the fact that it links up with the resuscitation taking place to-day.

I have already suggested that the attribution of clumsiness to Gothic artists (based on the fact that a neo-classical or Baroque sculptor, if his work resembled Gothic, would certainly have been clumsy) has assumed recently another form. We no longer call the mediaeval artists clumsy; judging, as usual, in the light of our own art, we call them "Expressionists." Uccello comes to the fore, while Guercino fades out. (How can anyone be interested in Guercino? After all, why not, considering that Velázquez was, and even bought his pictures for the King of Spain.)

In its process of retaining and revealing a forgotten art, every resuscitation casts great tracts of shadow over other aspects of the past. But the elect it favours and the sinners it condemns are parted by a blinding light, and no less than the place we now assign them, the values they formerly possessed undergo a reversal; thus for us to-day Uccello is neither what he was for his own age nor what he was for the eighteenth century; and the same applies to Guercino. We read into Titian more than we are willing to admit of Renoir; into Masaccio, of Cézanne; into El Greco, of the Cubists. And in Masaccio, as in El Greco, we exalt certain elements on which our choice has fallen, and ignore those which it rejects. True, we attempt to build a worthy memorial with all these fragments wrested from the past; but in terms of the modern soul, not of that of the past, and with an eye to the "noblest" conceptions the past can give us on our terms, not on its own. In 1910 it was assumed that the Winged Victory, when restored, would regain her ancient gold, her arms, her trumpet. Though none of these is hers to-day, she has regained her prow and, like a herald of the dawn, crowns the high stairway of the Louvre ; it is not towards Alexandria we have set her flight, but towards the Acropolis.

"Genius imposes on the ages a language constantly modified, like an echo answering each successive age with its own voice, and what the masterpiece keeps up is not a monologue, however authoritative, but a dialogue triumphant over Time."

NIKÉ ON HER NEW PEDESTAL

II It is impossible to understand the part played in our civilization by the resuscitations it has sponsored, if we fail to notice that this process of rediscovery began only when Christendom was entering on its decline. Not Christian faith, but Christendom; not religious thought, but that concept of a powerful religious structure moulding men's minds and souls, a last expression of which is to be found in those vestiges of their past retained by India, groping for her path, and Islam in its death-throes.

In his retreat at Port-Royal Racine was nearer to Saint Bernard than was an Encyclopaedist to Racine; for the very notion of "retreat" had ceased to mean anything to the Encyclopaedists. Man was in process of replacing the ideal of self-fulfilment through union with God, by the accumulation of multifarious knowledge; averting her interest from the human entity, Europe was on the way to becoming mistress of the world.

Whereas the most fertile emotions of the artists from the eleventh to the sixteenth century had been linked up with the substitution of at-one-ment with God for dualism, and of the human for the sacrosanct, creative art henceforth kept in step with the constant dwindling of the divine. Incapable of answering man's time-old questionings as to old age, death and the anomalies of his predicament, Christianity took the course of trying to forget them.

But first there came the Protestant upheaval and its sequels. In art this meant the pullulation of all visible forms, freed now from idealism; and these were called on to fill the void that even Rembrandt had failed to fill — that of Dutch painting.

We must begin by ridding ourselves of the notion that the Dutch of those days were "bourgeois," in the common meaning of the epithet. True, those who hailed with approval the evolution of their country's art from Hals's first canvases to the rise of the "Intimists" and genre-painters, were neither proletarians nor court dignitaries; but, where art is concerned, the term "bourgeois" conveys more than a social application. The men for whom Hals, Rembrandt, Ruysdael, Terborch, Vermeer and so many *petits maîtres* made their paintings had been the "sea-beggars," who had won their independence under Philip II or were about to defend it against Louis XIV. Victorious adversaries of the two mightiest kings of Europe, they were bourgeois like the Roundheads, not like Joseph Prudhomme. "They are quite ready to die for freedom. In their community none has a right to beat or even scold or roughly entreat another, and the serving-women have so many privileges that even their masters dare not strike them." The reward that Leiden chose for its courage when besieged was a university; so history tells us, and Taine dwelt lengthily on this. But we seem to have forgotten it. Is it not singular that even to-day we find people talking, as of quaint figures on picture-postcards, of a nation that put up an exemplary resistance to Hitler's hordes and has led the way in post-war reconstruction? If the Dutch grow tulips in the neighbourhood of Arnhem, those flowers are nourished by the bodies of many of their parachutists. Those to whom we would do best to relate the Dutch are the Scandinavians. But in them there is lacking a trait which neither the English, nor the Scandinavians, nor the Germans lack : a taste for the romantic — and, as a result, the faculty of weaving the stuff of dreams into their art.

Holland is ready enough to know the real, and God — but not that fringe of saints and heroes with whose glamour Italy had embellished Europe, and who were soon to seem no more than an august posterity of Van Dyck's portraits.

When the era of her great painting dawned, Holland, unlike Germany, had no compelling Gothic tradition. Indeed, she had no traditions; and, even to-day, the past has not in Holland the emphasis it has elsewhere. Her parachutists return, wearing the local costumes, to their homes in those old houses which look as if they had been built only yesterday. Amsterdam is the only seventeenth-century city — by rights it should have the "colour" of Versailles or Aachen — which it has been possible to repaint from roof-tree to cellar without a hint of vandalism, and which floats vague yet serene on Time's river. Romanticism (including that of Rubens' saints) being ruled out, nothing was left to the Dutch artist, so it then was said, but the portrait; an unjustified restriction, for within a few years, landscapes, still lifes and portraits were flourishing side by side. Or were the first-named regarded as "portraits" of the world? A Ruysdael landscape is hardly less transfigured than a Rembrandt, but in a different way. In any case Ruysdael and Rembrandt went to their graves unhonoured; at a pinch the Dutchman tolerates oak-trees' being "transfigured," but not his friends' faces. Real people — the butts in the comedies of such men as Steen and the Ostades are always nondescripts — must neither be idealized nor held up to ridicule. We talk of the plumes worn by Hals's models (who did not wear them long) and turn a blind eye to our own; we forget that while obviously these men are vain of their military equipment, they have as much right to take pride in it as had Cromwell's followers or the Russians of the first five-year plans.

"Our army is so good," the Venetians used to say, "that any one of our common soldiers could be captain in an Italian army, and an Italian captain would not be accepted by us as a private soldier." In Hals's last portraits there is a grandiose vindictiveness; but as for irony, it is we who foist it on them. He did not laugh at these people whom he was so far from seeing as romantic heroes. What was dying in Holland in those days was the Italianate way of seeing Man.

Or, rather, it may be said, the Catholic way of seeing him. Still Protestantism in art did not run on lines parallel to Catholicism. There is a drab, bourgeois type of Protestant portrait, which never rises above the second rank. But, by its very nature,

Protestantism did not aim at any equivalent of the great Catholic world order; nor did it aim at building another St Peter's. In Protestant and, at the same time, monarchical England, it was the monarchy that set the portrait's tone. The Reformation wished to restore to St Augustine's voice its dark reverberations, and make good the prerogative of individual man; Reformation and monarchy alike repudiated the Roman hierarchy.

True, the Primitives and the masters of the Renaissance had painted landscapes, still lifes and interiors (subjects which Holland multiplied and valued for their own sakes), but they set little store by them, as being mere by-products. For them, such subjects had no point unless they served some higher end. The Dutch were not the first to paint a fish on a plate; but they were the first to cease treating it as food for the apostles. Caravaggio had recently indulged in a form of realism which, though it no longer felt called on to idealize each figure, remained subject to the Italian hierarchy, and all he asked of it was that it should express more vividly the presence of an ideal world. In the *Madonna of the Ostlers* he covers Saint Anne's face with wrinkles whose function is to impart to her daughter's face a purity different no doubt from Raphael's, but no less intense. And even the few still lifes he made seem decorations for some unseen composition from which he has forcibly detached them. Until now, all forms of realism had (as had early Gothic realism) aimed at suggesting the presence of the invisible, particularly of incidents connected with the life of Christ; thus Bosch's torturers, the Master of Alkmaar's beggars are inseparable from Christ, whether He be present in, or absent from, the picture. But in the canvases of Hals and Terborch neither Christ nor beauty has a place. True, the social order for which Dutch painting catered dictated its themes and mood; nevertheless the genius of the great Dutch painters ranged far beyond these limits. Hals is not an improved Van der Helst, Vermeer is not a refined version of Pieter de Hooch (not to mention Rembrandt). The fact that the tradition of the portrait was so strong in the Netherlands made for a rapid development of the highest craftsmanship in this field. But a portrait is more than a reproduction of a face; in a social order no less averse from Spanish austerity than from the dazzling sensuality of Venice, how could a great painter have expressed his genius save by discovering a new scale of "values" in the portrait?

With Hals began — if with a show of diffidence — that new relationship, one of rivalry, between the painter and his model, which Manet was the first to bring into the open. Like Rubens (they were almost contemporaries), he took over together with their colour (which indeed owed something to the North) the broad brushstrokes of the Venetians. But in Venetian art these *served* the model, elevating the human element, across the haze of broken lights of the last Titians, towards a God soon to become a Jesuit God; much as they swept the Flemish peasantry, indeed the whole visible world, into Rubens' Bacchanalia. Kings had been a favoured theme with Titian and Rubens, who imparted to their faces a touch of regal grandeur. But grandeur was no longer sought after; Hals's brushstroke does not glorify his model, but transmutes him into painting.

Rembrandt, who owed little to him, faced the same problem. But his Protestantism is not a more or less rationalized Catholicism; in his own way, and in the exact meaning of the word, he is a Prophet. A God-possessed man, brother to Dostoevsky, and fraught with the future — a future he does not announce, but bears within him, as the Hebrew prophets bore within them the advent of Christ, and as he bore within himself the past. For it was not the picturesqueness of the Jewish legends that attracted him, nor the past they stood for — but the element of the eternal. A convert, an outlaw less by reason of his deeds than in his soul, a lover of servant-girls, one of whom went mad (a son of Hals, too, died in an asylum), he waged war, with all the might of his genius, against the world of appearances and a social order in which he saw but a blind wall separating him from Christ. In his parleyings with the angel who alternately crushes and forsakes him, the earth becomes a void in which only two figures, Christ and himself, exist; and he is not Mynheer Rembrandt Harmenszoon, but an embodiment of all those miseries of man's estate but for which Christ's voice would serve no end. It was by way of man, the individual, that the Reformation was to hear that voice again; and Rembrandt was obsessed by his own face which, to begin with, he portrayed under many guises — not (as some have said) to beautify it, but to multiply its intimations — and from which, in a later phase, derived the women's faces, painted by him, which have their family likeness because they all are like himself. Indeed we seem to see his features (which bring Molière's to mind) glimmering even through those of Christ in the "Hundred-Guilder Print."

He is not only a painter; he is one of the few religious poets of the West. That is why his painting, which does not illustrate his poetry but expresses it, encountered (once he gave it full expression) a bitterer resistance than Franz Hals had to face. The failure of *The Night Watch* was inevitable. Captain Banning Cocq and his brother officers wished to have their portraits painted, admiring as they did that not too independent canvas *Dr Tulp's Anatomy Lesson,* and commissioned Rembrandt for this task. But he did not paint their portraits, which did not interest him in the least; there was not the stuff of a picture in Cocq giving the order to "turn out the guard." Instead, he brought together an oddly miscellaneous group, in which figured not only the officers but a dwarf and one of those women of his who seem to have stepped out of the Bible : a world whose light and shade seem the stuff of music, and which tends already towards that world, soon to be his, where God is omnipresent. Unfortunately for the painter,

REMBRANDT. THE NIGHT WATCH

the pasty-faced Goyesque "hero" into which he transformed the officer who stands beside the Captain was not at all to that worthy's liking; he had wanted to cut a stately figure, not to be shepherded with his patrol into a vision of Judgement Day!

In short, these Dutch militia officers expected him to give them their "Sunday faces," as Van der Helst (on whom, in fact, they fell back after this disappointment) would have done. They failed to realize that Rembrandt's Sunday was not theirs. With the Venetians idealization had not meant truckling to ignoble vanity, but the very essence of their art. A comparison of Tintoretto's noble portraits (at the Venice Academy) with those of Rembrandt brings this out. Portraiture for Rembrandt meant neither idealization nor rendering an expression; his genius, which had no truck with psychology, has for its symbol that *Woman Sweeping,* who is not even humble and, if confronted with Christ, would have made the most poignant Woman of Samaria ever painted.

40

It is strange indeed that the mightiest response to men's vast yearning for human fellowship should be the dialogue of a soul with God. This was the truth that Rembrandt discovered in his art. And, at the very time when non-religious painting was coming to the fore, he alone — with hands that tremblingly grasped once more the mantle of Him who walked beside the travellers on the road to Emmaus — upheld that truth among men. But his art, which had no predecessors, had likewise no successors. Lastman, Elsheimer, like Bol and Aart de Gelder, have much of his manner, but nothing of his incommunicable genius. We have only to compare the touches of Old Testament picturesqueness in the work of Lastman, his teacher, or Elsheimer's *Flight into Egypt* with his, to realize that between him and these there lies — a Revelation !

But this seventeenth-century Michelangelo had no Pope Julius II ; his reverent praise of God did not extend to glorification of the world, still less of its grandees. Nor could his biblical personages find a home in Protestant churches, which excluded "images." The heroic age of Protestantism was running its course in a land where Protestantism was now the birthright of all, no longer the outcome of a personal resolve ; and his isolated pictures had a less compelling impact on his contemporaries than has his work, as a whole, on us. To carry on his task (as to carry on Dostoevsky's), what would have been needed was not only a great painter, but also a spirit akin to his and capable, like his, of forging for itself the language of its dialogue with Christ. Another Tolstoi — a successor, not a follower. But none was to be to him what Tintoretto was for Titian. To make good, the Protestant painter of those days needed either to have genius or to make shift with values of a non-spiritual order, to belong to the aristocratic school of English painting, or the middle-class of Dutch. The Reformation, and the changes in the world order leading up to it, had driven him out of cover ; expelled from the world of the sacrosanct, he was now plunged into a world, still in the making, of the "profane," and this was to be his contribution to European art.

These *petits maîtres* were already in the saddle when Rembrandt was dying, forsaken by all. For many centuries his unquiet spirit was to haunt the museums, telling these lesser men what they lacked. They claimed to put "reality" on to canvas ; but, apart from landscape, all they brought to art was some slight enlargement of the tavern-scene, the anecdote, the dining-room, the frivolous. One is surprised by the narrow range of their subjects and their repetitiveness, though this indeed was inevitable, since talent as opposed to genius limits themes no less than their treatment. What they discovered was the *emptiness* of the world — mitigated by the pathetic fallacy, as is the way with art that aspires merely to adorn. Yet these "little masters" were capable of painting excellent pictures ; its exemption from romantic tradition freed their art from any propensity to "glamourous" effect. One of them, indeed, proved that a man of genius could vie with Rembrandt, though seeming to restrict himself to the world of Pieter de Hooch, by bringing out what Hals had strongly, Terborch obscurely, adumbrated, a fact which Rembrandt's genius, haunted by the absolute, had been unwilling to accept : the fact that an artist, standing by himself, can rescue painting from a world that has no intrinsic value, by ascribing to *painting itself* an intrinsic value.

The sociologist sees Vermeer as merely one more "Intimist" or genre-painter ; not so the artist. At thirty he was already tiring of the anecdote, and in Dutch painting the anecdote plays a leading part. The honestly felt sentimentalism of his fellow-artists was alien to him ; the climate of his art is poetic and due above all to its refinement. His technique is as different from that of Pieter de Hooch, to whose it used to be assimilated (we have only to compare their treatment of leafage and, especially, of the pictures they place on the walls of their interiors), as from that of Terborch or even the best of Fabritius. He was little closer to them than was Cézanne to the school of *pleinairistes.*

The confusion has arisen from his taking over subjects from their school ; those painters who are nearest akin to him, Chardin and Corot, were to treat theirs with like indifference. But in these "borrowings" he kept his distance ; his anecdotes are not really anecdotes, his atmospheres are not mere atmosphere, his sentiment is not sentimental, his scenes are hardly scenes, twenty of the forty pictures known to us contain only one figure and yet they are not quite portraits in the ordinary sense. He always seems to disindividualize his models, just as he strips his world of particulars, not so as to create types, but, rather, an extremely sensitive abstraction which brings to mind certain Greek *Korés.* The modelling he practises is not Hooch's sentimental modelling, linked up with appearances and depth. Often, he uses a sort of "levelling out" which acts as a response to some other part of the picture. Thus the smooth water in the *View of Delft* is an "answer" to the tiles and glittering barges ; the face of the *Young Girl* to the shadows of her turban, so clean-cut that we see the brushstrokes ; the bodice of the *Young Lady in Blue,* to the chairs' dark blue patches ; the shadow in the *Woman weighing Pearls,* to the pearls themselves, and to the young woman's face, worthy of Piero della Francesca. How easy is it for us now, when we contemplate that face, to see the genius hidden for two centuries beneath craftsmanship lavish to the point of prodigality and under a consciously sought-after charm ! In this picture the masses are subjected to that bold simplification which imparts to the *Young Girl* its effect of some translucent stone smoothed by the sea ; to the expressions of his models, their suggestiveness, and to his flatter figures their affinity to Corot's figures. In this discreetly stylized treatment of volumes — the date is 1660 — distance is ignored. There has been talk about the "vistas" in the *View of Delft* and the *Street in Delft.* Actually, when we examine the originals

VERMEER. WOMAN WEIGHING PEARLS (DETAIL)

VERMEER.   A STREET IN DELFT

HOBBEMA.   THE AVENUE

— which contrast in this respect with so many contemporary canvases in the Rijks-museum and Mauritshuis — we are struck by their lay-out in large planes perpendicular to the spectator, and notched as to their edges.   Whereas the landscapes, even the urban views, are frankly perspectives.   (Hobbema was but a few years junior to him, and there is a vast gap between the *View of Delft* and the long recession of the *Avenue*.)   Like his best figures, his landscapes triumph over Space in quite the modern manner, and this is what gives the *Street in Delft,* as against so many pictures built with the same bricks, its imperishable style.   A style less compelling and revealing in the *Head of a Young Girl* than in *The Love-Letter,* which is certainly one of Vermeer's last canvases, less famous than the others because of its less obvious charm.

The setting is an abstract ground in which the door (despite the oblique line) links up with the curtain, the chair and the wall, which almost merge into each other.   The

"Intimists" would have treated this spatial recession corridor-wise, following the canons of a set perspective, and with regressive values; Vermeer treats the wall at the back as a backcloth impermeable as a shutter. Between two planes, within a space described by some as "cubist," he paints the servant, to whom the broad sweep of the style and the intensity of the tones give the solidity of a caryatid, and the woman playing the guitar, whose paradoxically massive lightness and almost bovine gaze make us forget that her face is built up like those of the *Young Woman at a Casement* and the *Woman weighing Pearls*. The tiles extending from the door to the two women, and harmonizing so well with the sandals and domestic objects which create a well-defined depth, seem the very symbol of the work. The letter has no importance, and the women none. Nor has the concrete world in which the letter is being delivered; for that world has been transmuted into painting.

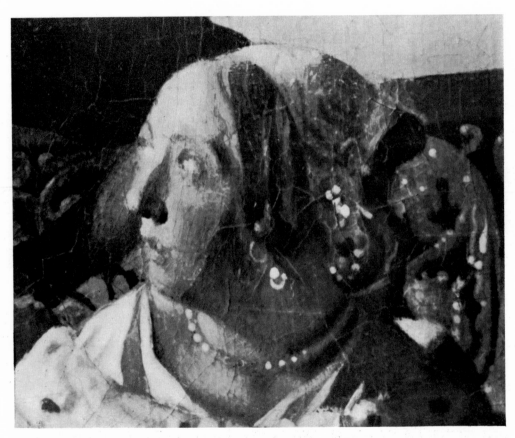

VERMEER. THE LOVE LETTER (DETAIL)

All the same, modern art had not yet begun. For this transmutation of the world into painting, far from being openly announced, partakes in Vermeer's art (as in Velázquez' *Las Meninas*) of the nature of a secret. Reality is not subordinated to painting; on the contrary painting seems the handmaid of reality, though groping towards some treatment which is neither subject to appearances nor yet in conflict with them, a balanced

compromise. Actually, however, painting had never been governed by appearances, but by a notion of values, almost always transcendental in their nature, which shaped its ends. (This is overlooked only if painting is regarded *primarily* as the record of visual experience.) In 1670 Hals and Rembrandt were dead, and an epoch died with them. Vermeer, with another five years of life before him, inaugurated a new epoch. Two centuries were to pass before this fact was realized.

But Velázquez, too, was dead; as were Van Dyck and Poussin. Now that the Protestant illumination, after having brought the landscape into view, was reduced to a

VELAZQUEZ. ISABEL DE VELASCO (DETAIL FROM LAS MENINAS)

gleam of candlelight, the gradual eclipse of the divine element in the Catholic world progressed through vast, successive zones of shadow. And, as we have seen, a circumstance without precedent was that, for the first time, a religion was not being threatened by the birth of another religion; what was now disappearing from the Western world was the Absolute.

The glimmer of the little oil-lamps affixed to the walls of the Catacombs had sufficed to make, for those who came up from that realm of shadows, the blaze of light in the Roman upper-world seem like a madmen's carnival. Would they have regarded otherwise the Rome of the eighteenth century? Here there is no question of the form assumed by a religion, but one of that impulse of the soul which, wresting man from his mundane life, unites him with the Eternal. Athirst for personal salvation, the West forgets that many religions had but a casual vision of the life beyond the grave; true, all great religions stake their claim on Eternity, but not necessarily on man's eternal life.

In those Oriental religions which are best known to us the links with Eternity are plain to see; are they less evident in Buddhism, with its insistence on the Wheel (so as to escape from it for ever), or in Brahmanism, which is rooted in Eternity? The anti-religious mood of the eighteenth century looked for precursors; but though there had been Greek sceptics, there had never been a culture pledged to scepticism (and ours is not sponsored by our agnosticism, but by our conquest of the world). Confucianism, cautious as it is, needs its Son of Heaven. Venus envelops all in a caress that knows no end; Amphitrite merges in the ocean all men and their generations, drifting past like ripples on the water's face. With the possible exception of Roman culture, all early cultures left the clearest token of their significance in the gestures of a passionate attempt to compass their eternity.

But now eternity withdrew itself from the world. And our culture became as unresponsive to the voice of Christianity as to the Druid trees. We have heard too much talk of the "decadences" of antiquity, in which that cry "Great Pan is dead!" made a horde of half-prostrate gods spring to their feet, in futile protest; for us the Eternal in its death-throes was not replaced by any sorry substitute, until an adversary that at least was worthy of it had been discovered. For now the only enemy of the Eternal which the human mind has ever found was set up in its stead: and that enemy is — history.

But history is a construction of the mind, and forms deriving from an interpretation of the past have not the same weight as those by means of which man once freed himself from Time. Inasmuch as it is only when the deepest layers of their personality are involved that artists embark on a metamorphosis of forms, the passing of the absolute in art was bound to be attended by upheavals of much violence. The surprising thing is not that art was affected by this passing of the absolute, but that it was not affected more. One reason is that many centuries had gone to the discovery of the forms of Christendom, and the losing of them was likewise a slow process. Also, the Christians and their antagonists lived side by side (like the Catholics and Protestants). Rembrandt's art did not destroy Rubens', nor Courbet's art that of Delacroix. And some of those who were seeking the new language of the secret places of the heart fancied themselves the bitterest enemies of Christ. Finally, though conflict does not replace the absolute, it helps men to forget it.

The heat and dust of the war the philosophers were waging against the church obscured for them the limits of that which they thought they were waging against Christ. Despite the common belief, the eighteenth century was not a sceptical age; it was combative, and in foisting on the world a "Goddess of Reason," it showed its hand.

What was being substituted for the Christian order it assailed, was not so much the values which were used as slogans, as the fervour generated by the very vehemence of this attack. (In many cases what was being attacked was not the Christian faith, but a piety from which all sacred elements had disappeared.) And painting could not have its Voltaire; it is easier to body forth a *Mérope* than a *Candide* in terms of plastic art. Soon the emotions uniting all men — piety, sensual pleasure, and the like — tended to oust the unity imposed by the Christian order. But the painters were far less involved in the struggle in progress than were the philosophers.

They were "war values" that enabled Reason to replace the absolute by exaltation; for emotions centering on the people, the nation — anyhow in times of conflict — are forms of communion. Thus the soldiers of Year II were held to be the successors of the crusaders, while the Nation and the French People took the place of God. The symbols and passions of a political system linking up with Rousseau led yet again to the substitution for a Church of that which claimed to be a Gospel. The political deity of the xixth century, modelled no less on human values than on the gods of Greece, stepped into the place, though with a very different mien, of the Jesuits' God. And soon emitted the same hollow sound.

"The world has been empty since the Romans!" Saint-Just might have phrased it more accurately: "Let the world be full, as in Roman times, so that the men of my kind may live in it!" Louis David fixed his eyes on Romans who fitted in, more or less, with the Empire. But already the limits of political exaltation were growing apparent. It was not in France that the hinge of the century was being hammered into shape; true, he who heard anew that ancient voice was a "man of the Enlightenment" — but that man was Goya.

Though the *Shootings of May 3* is imbued with notions of the People, of Justice and the Nation, its whole outlook links up with many *Crucifixions*. For the underground world in which at the time art was striking root was very different from that obvious domain lit by the sun of Reason.

"The horses of death are beginning to neigh . . ." Like Hugo and Goya, Byron, Schiller, Michelet — and also Goethe — were creators of monsters. Hugo's genius (even if we disregard Gilliat's octopus) reaches out, like Booz, into a cosmic realm peopled with elemental forms, the raw material, as it were, of the sacrosanct. And art subsists more through that on which it feeds than by its "message."

That so many great poets, and likewise great minds — Nerval, Baudelaire, Goethe, Dostoevsky — were at a certain period so much addicted to the "diabolical" gives food for thought; yet Spain realized that Goya's genius began when the horned devil was transmuted into the spectre of the tortured man.

When the Revolution and the Nation, followed by Science, had lost that prestige of the absolute which nineteenth-century optimism had bestowed on them, there began that incapacity of modern civilization for giving forms to its spiritual values. Even if these come from Rome. There where once soared a cathedral, men fall to feebly building a pseudo-romanesque or pseudo-gothic church; or else the modern church, in which Christ is not. Remained the Mass said on the mountain-top, to whose perils and equivocations the Church soon became alive; in our time the only setting worthy of itself that the Mass found was within the barbed wire of the camps.

It is perhaps significant that Christianity, which still delivers dying men from the sting of death, and alone gives form (in the highest sense of the term) to their last end, fails to give its churches a style enabling Christ to figure in them otherwise than as an intruder; and likewise fails, in its portrayal of saints, to unite the communion of saints with artistic excellence. Here we have more than the mere conflict between religion and individualism; for if the community of believers came to be really moved by Rouault's art, they would assuredly be moved by the art of the Middle Ages, and the Church would acclaim, before a *Descent from the Cross* by Rouault, the Villeneuve *Pietà*. This conflict is apparent wherever machine-age culture has made good. Only where they are unscathed by it have Islam, India and China preserved their religious forms; not at Cairo, Bombay or Shanghai. And no new forms are found to replace these. Surely that little pseudo-Gothic church on Broadway, tucked away amongst the skyscrapers, is symbolic of the age! On the whole face of the globe the civilization that has conquered it has failed to build a temple or a tomb.

Agnosticism is no novelty; it is an agnostic civilization that is new. Whether Cesare Borgia believed in God or not, he reverently bore the holy relics; while he was blaspheming amongst his cronies, St Peter's was being built. The art of a living religion is not that of an insurance against death, but one of man's defense against fatality by a vast communion.

Our civilization has been the first in recorded time to be unaware of this transcendent communion linking each man to his fellow men, and to all the forms of sorrow, all the forms of life (whether "sentimental" or metaphysical); but we are beginning to be aware of it. The individual made his appearance late in history. It was neither he, nor the Supreme Being, that Robespierre set up against Christ; it was the Nation he set up. The individual thrown back on himself perceives that he does not amount to much; and that the "supermen" who once fired his enthusiasm had all a large slice of common humanity. But an individualism that goes beyond mere hedonism has difficulty in resisting the lure of grandeur. The myth of Man (which preceded that of the individual and survived it) is affected in the same way. The question "Is man dead?" implies an affirmation that he is Man and not his recrement, in so far as he aspires to building himself up in terms of what is loftiest in him and is rarely limited to himself.

A culture based on man, the individual, seldom lasts long, and eighteenth-century rationalism culminated in that outburst of passionate hope which has left its mark on history; but the culture of that century summoned back to life whatever in the past endorsed its rationalism, whereas ours resuscitates all that sponsors our irrationalism.

NEW GUINEA. SKULL STAND

III The transformation of Negro masks — objects serving as the "vehicles" of spirits — into works of cubist sculpture was one of the most suggestive metamorphoses of our time; it was only later that we took notice of their magical properties. While to the modern artist these works sponsored by our "anti-Renaissance" present themselves as systems of forms, our culture has regarded them on different lines: sometimes as indictments, almost always as challenges to the established order of our world.

To begin with, we have products of the various popular arts, from the descriptive art of the picture-sheets to that of the wayside crucifix. These creations were no more accidental than were those of the masters; their makers knew their public. This, where an art of the rich exists alongside, is a typical poor man's art. Attuned to the simplified forms familiar to the peasantry, it draws on their legendary lore, whose roots plunge deep in Time; and in every "sheet of saints" there is something of the ikon. Copper-plate engraving was costly, the cabinet picture still more costly. The humble of the earth may not have felt themselves rejected by the Jesuit pictures, but they certainly felt they were by Poussin, Watteau, Gainsborough. The popular effigy or picture-sheet,

anyhow, did not humiliate them. Still, though the sentimentalism of the masses was gratified by a form of expression that seemed made to their measure, it appreciated other forms of expression, provided they too were sentimental. As soon as reproductions entered on the scene, it became clear that the peasantry did not necessarily prefer a crudely naïve style; Georgin's successor on the walls of village inns was not some Breton folk artist, but Detaille, and the successors of those who carved the wayside crosses were the statue-moulders of Saint-Sulpice.

In the period when modern art was born (round about 1860) popular art was on its way to extinction, along with the Midsummer Night's fires, Carnival and the maypoles, and it made its entry into the artists' world at the very moment of its dying out. It had broken away from aristocratic art, when a non-religious culture had overlaid that of Christendom, and it remained linked up with Gothic art in so far as this art expressed emotions that it shared. The "Protat Woodcut" is the small change, so to speak, of the great Gothic art, but Georgin is not that of Delacroix. It was not due to chance that

PROTAT WOODCUT (CA. 1460)

56

the folk-picture makers kept stubbornly to Giotto's "gentil knights" (to whom — who knows? — we may one day return). And the Épinal colour-sheets for popular consumption replaced biblical themes with . . . Napoleon. Linked up as are all popular arts with legendary religious lore, it is above all in Europe that they seem to retain the Gothic idiom. And, once another idiom, that of Celtic coins (which seems to go back to prehistory and belongs perhaps to the great migrations), had died out, popular art throughout Europe tended towards a still more naïvely primitive script, that of the butter-mould and the gingerbread cake, common to both Slavs and Westerners. This is the humble

SWISS FOLK ART. MOULD

décor of those forms of poverty and human suffering whose depths were plumbed by Gothic art. Indeed its most widely known (though not its most successful) works suggest to us, if wrongly, that all popular art is vaguely Gothic — a suggestion emanating solely from our European works of art. To Chinese popular art the style of our shepherd's crooks is practically unknown; Africa and Polynesia add their characteristic angles; the pictures Islam gives us to-day are pure calligraphy. What connects Gothic with a certain type of popular art which seems to us (unjustifiably) to symbolize all such arts, is its combination of sentimentality and stiffness. Neither the popular art of Asia, nor the Gheber pottery in which we find that rare thing, a hint of a Byzantine popular art, has

any tendency towards a broken line or flutings. In Central Europe the arabesque, which, by way of Baroque, entered into popular art, ceases to express depth and movement, and develops a sinuosity sometimes like that of the East, or a childishly poetic calligraphy; it contrasts loosely flowing curves with geometrical patterns far more rudimentary than Gothic patterns, and its drawing often reminds us more of Dufy than of mediaeval

POLISH FOLK ART

POLISH FOLK ART

CZECH FOLK ART (1844)

woodcuts. Whatever be their linear patterns, popular arts seek to preserve that expression of the past which is threatened by the forms of civilization, whence aristocratic art arises — an expression of that uncharted sea of time across which civilizations, like lost armadas, glide into oblivion. These forms draw all the "historical" arts whence they arise towards the same depths, where they merge saints and knights of old, Cartouche, Mandrin, Judith, the Robin Hoods of folklore, in a system of forms tending to the volute, and of a stiffness for which the woodblock is not sufficient to account. We most clearly see this process at work in Breton art, which produced works of an almost monumental order, whose chronology we know. Its famous "Calvaries" began during the Renaissance, and have kept up their struggle against it ever since. Their figures seek to take

"CALVARY" AT PLEYBEN (XVIth AND XVIIth CENT.).   THE MAGI

over those of the royal tombs ; alongside the immemorial peasant faces and those of
apostles — the poor relations of those wonderful pre-Romanesque figures of Auvergne —
we see plumed feudal lords whose rigidity suggests a transposition, on heavier lines,
of Spain ; the same lines as those which were soon, in the near-by churches, to impose
their heaviness on the dancing, golden grace of Italy.

The popular handling of colour (as in those doll-like figurines known in Provence
as "santons") is no less different from the colour of the art museum than is popular
drawing from academic ; far more than its forms, whose borrowings are often unmis-
takable, the colour of popular art is something quite independent, a law unto itself. The

earlier Provençal santons are so much like little shapeless blobs that when modern santon-makers, wishing to convert them into statuettes, took to giving them real faces, their distinctive quality is lost. Like that of the old colour-prints, though more subtly, their colour is neither Romanesque nor Gothic, but rather that of the turquoise-and-coral plaques of the lands of snow; of the glassware trinkets of savage races, their feather-jewellery and ceremonial costumes — one of the world's oldest "languages." These arts appertain to a culture distant in Time instead of being distant in Space, and to the mystery-play (and the Punch-and-Judy show), but not to the theatre. For us to get from them more than a rather grudging pleasure, all that they need is that spark of immortality inseparable from genius.

Herein lies, it seems, the difference between folk art and naïve art. The former has its traditions, strict as those of academic art. Usually it is the language of one particular artist, addressed to a special public; Georgin could have easily engraved, not to say drawn, academic battlepieces. Yet the forms of naïve art also obey a tradition which we would be rash in attributing to naïvety alone. Even in 1950, they hardly dare to dispense with the up-curled moustache. Is it to be believed that "Sunday painters" at the close of the XIXth century, when they showed persons resembling not so much waxwork figures as manne-quins, did not know what they were about? The painters at coun-try fairs knew well what subjects were expected of them (ranging from the *Crocodile River* to soldiers and wedding-scenes, from Jules Verne to Déroulède), and what style to follow. We need only compare these naïve works with those of Persia and China, or with the figures Islam is now beginning to countenance in its Mediter-ranean seaports. To define the limits set to instinct in the various types of popular art we need only contrast the figures made by Catho-lic Slavs with those of Orthodox Slavs; a mere sixty miles — but

NAÏVE PERSIAN ART (EARLY XXth CENT.)

SLAV FOLK ART (ORTHODOX). XIXth CENTURY

two schools of painting differing from time immemorial — separate a Pole from a Russian even more than from a Breton. And naïve Russian art resembles that of the ikons, not that of the Douanier Rousseau.

In this connection, the "case" of this remarkable artist is worth considering. Did the Douanier paint, in all innocence, just what he saw? We know his drawings and sketches, in which the care for detail we associate with him is absent. Whether clumsy

HENRI ROUSSEAU.   SKETCH FOR "THE AVENUE"

or not (and, on occasion, extremely clumsy), the style of his major works was as pur-
posively worked up as was Van Eyck's. He admired Bouguereau, we are told? It is
not great artists who paint like those they admire; it is the clever artists. To perceive
that the *Snake Charmer*, the *Parc Montsouris* and *Summer* are elaborately composed works,
we need only rid ourselves of the preconception that naïvety is *in itself* creative and
study them between, for instance, any truly naïve picture and Uccello's *Story of the
Host*. "People have told me," the Douanier wrote in 1910, "that my work does not
belong to this age. Surely you will understand that at this stage I cannot change my
manner, which is the result of long years of persistent research." A look at his sketches —
a jumble of patches — is enough to convince us that, though certainly there was in
Rousseau the stuff of a naïve painter, he wrested his true style from this, bit by bit.

Let us ignore the second-rate, which bulks large in his output: over-simplified
landscape, conventional lay-figures. He is a painter to be treated anthologically (as
indeed all modern painting should be treated, more or less). And the same holds good

HENRI ROUSSEAU. SUMMER

for the masters of the past, where world-famous names conjure up for us, not the by-products of a studio, but a limited number of supreme masterworks. The Douanier's best pictures reveal a great colourist, whose colour is anything but naïve. The garish hues of popular or folk pictures are absent from it, and usually the harmonies are discreet, even if sometimes they tend towards tonal combinations which have a popular appeal — those of uniforms, for instance. But you will never find the blue of the *Wedding* and *The Poet and his Muse,* or the white of *The Tollhouse,* in bric-à-brac shops ; nor the colours of *The Snake Charmer,* in which the yellow edging of the irises is by no means realistic. Only when his best pictures are reproduced in black and white are they liable to be confused with naïve art ; never when we see the pictures themselves. The naïve painters lived on the margin of the art world ; whereas Rousseau counted painters and poets amongst his friends, and we can arrange his works chronologically in most cases, as we do those of famous artists. But of the naïve painters who preceded him (and even those who followed him) we know only isolated works. More noteworthy still : at a time when poetry and painting seemed to have parted company, he renewed that incantation which we find in Piero di Cosimo and which was to reappear in Chirico, but is no longer heard. And perhaps Apollinaire would have responded less readily to that age-old colour magic, had not a certain poetic accent, to which the poet in himself responded, whispered to him of genius.

True, there is little or nothing of the child — visibly, anyhow — in the great poets ; yet, no one who has come in contact with several cannot have failed to recognize the type, at once infantile, forceful and withal a shade sophisticated, to which they belong. There is more than a touch of Verlaine in the Douanier. Those young writers who thought they were "pulling the old boy's leg" were to hear echoing in their inner ear long after his death, the waltzes played by his faithful shade. They called on him, "just to have a good laugh" (so they said, untruthfully) ; they were to be the builders of his fame. Even had he never painted a canvas, a man who could gather under Picasso's roof — comic as the occasion may have seemed — Apollinaire, Braque, Salmon and Gertrude Stein, was clearly someone to be taken seriously, to say the least of it. When, by way of a joke, some art students sent a man dressed up as Puvis de Chavannes to call on him, he calmly replied : "I was expecting you." It was only in the manner of Dostoevsky's "Idiot" that the name fitted this simpleton of genius. "There is a terrible power in humility."

The Douanier is less a naïve artist than the exponent of an immemorial language. I heard the last great Lesghy poet recite his poems ; no one in the room understood his language, yet poets of ten nations felt the air vibrant with a message from the dark abysm of time. Rousseau's roots lay in that half-forgotten underworld. Had he not been able to paint his virgin forests, he would have rendered his suburban scenes quite

differently. In the *Hungry Lion* of 1905, he harks back to that theme of animals fighting which obtained for four millennia, from Sumer to Alexandria, and is found even at the foot of the Great Wall. And above the lion which he did not see in Mexico (where there are none) he sets the owl of the Zoological Gardens, an ancient symbol of the devil. Thus his greatest paintings link up with the unrecorded past.

TETRADRACHM OF AKANTHUS

His endless childhood — like real childhood — is haunted by atavistic memories. And this is why, far more than by virtue of his forms (though such obsession calls for certain forms), his art reaches out far beyond his "Sundayfied" painting, into the farthest hinterlands of popular art. We find again those animals of his done in flat planes, sometimes dark and sometimes white but always of a wraithlike hue, in the American

"Primitives" — in the *Horse* at the Whitney Museum, the *Buffalo Hunter* at Santa Barbara. By reason of that poetic feeling which, by lifting some of his canvases far above a style puerile at first sight, forces us to see them *all,* and by reason of the sublimated emotion of others ; by his colour, and by a systematized handling of form (in *Summer, Les Buttes-Chaumont* and several landscapes) as remote from the art of his time as from that of the folk artists — by all these means he recalled to life the latter, much as (on a far larger scale, of course) the men of the Renaissance resuscitated the art of Antiquity. Such indeed is the prerogative of all creative art. And thus on evenings when he felt particularly depressed, the grey hair of the lonely widower playing his flute before the *Portrait of Clemence, My Wife,* was lightly, soothingly caressed by that august hand with which Michelangelo roused the *Laocoön* from its slumbers, and in his humble studio in Plaisance that primitive tune, played by the *Snake Charmer,* too, conjured up the world's oldest dreams.

For the "resurrection" of naïve painting Rousseau was not indispensable ; the Primitives would have sufficed. Nevertheless, he drew it in his train, as once the Masters

drew their disciples after them ; and this *ignotus* who signs his work, this "innocent" patronized by a knowing few, has taken his due place in the lineage of art, as did the abstract painters, successors of the Cubists. Dead, the Douanier became leader of a school. But his true school was not that of the naïve imitators who followed him. For he was not naïve, but a seer ; though he measured the noses of his sitters, his art, meticulous in detail, is as fantastic as that of Bosch. It was not conditioned by what he actually saw (though Impressionism was in its heyday ; Rousseau was only twelve years younger than Manet), but by what he wished to do ; it is his escape from "the wheel" of art-history, felt by us as a deliverance, that brings him into line with our resuscitations ; and not his so-called naïvety, which was but the price he paid for this escape.

If we have difficulty in making this distinction, the reason is that, in our resuscitations, the elements due to the trend of modern art and those due to our present taste are so inextricably mingled.

Though we should obviously be wrong in regarding modern art as being wholly ruled by taste, the satisfaction of sensibility for its own sake plays a considerable part in it. Symptomatic of what is happening is something of which we see no trace in older painting and which, for want of a better name, we may call the "patch." A patch that is neither worked into the structure of the picture nor into its composition in the traditional meaning of that term ; nor is it a stress laid on any detail of execution or, as in Japan, on some detail of portrayal. It now seems to exist capriciously, in its own right. Yet almost always in the work of those who inaugurated it, a link can be detected ; in the case of Picasso, with a passionate constructivism ; in Bonnard's case, then Braque's, with an effect of harmony ; in Léger's, with an architectural set-up. Sometimes, too, the "patch" strikes a subtle yet high-pitched note keyed to the script (perceptible from Dufy onwards to André Masson's blotches of blood-red). But with Miró, as formerly with Kandinsky and at times with Klee, all such subordination of the "patch" is done away with ; we are tempted to speak of a one-dimensional art. Indeed this fascination of the "patch" seems to incite the painter to blot out the picture itself (as it does the calligraphy in some of Picasso's work). In Picasso's case as in Miró's, it pointed the way to ceramics ; indeed it seems to spring from a wish for some pictorial outlet other than the picture. Here there is no question of decorative art ; it is a far cry from these earthenware objects to what some gay vase painted by Renoir might have been, or to the tapestry designs made by Poussin, or to Goya in his first phase. "You can eat off them," Picasso says, pointing to his plates, knowing quite well that most are made for preventing people's eating off them. This accidental, tempestuous, dazzling art of his brings to mind those darkly glowing patches on some kinds of Persian crockery, above all when it has come to us in fragments. (Like those on the Koum vases, the modern patch is associated with a fine-spun, sometimes naïve linework, seemingly quite out of keeping, yet in fact developing its fullest value when brought in contact with the patch.) In such cases these Persian patches make their impression on our minds without reference to the object to which they once belonged, and which we should never have thought of comparing with a picture. Thus we can use them for weighing up the picture; but not (apter though this might seem) the so-called *objet d'art*.

True, art has often redrawn its frontiers, and the basic stuff of a work of plastic art is not necessarily painting. Nevertheless we are not concerned here with a new birth like that of the stained-glass window. We are touching on what is (for the time being) the extreme limit of our modern painting, standing in relation to our culture as does the "savage" cloak of feathers, which in fact is justified by the patch; for the modern artist has taken over the fetish and incorporated it in his art. An "absolutely free" art does not lead to the picture or the statue, but to *objects*.

These objects which are making their surreptitious way into our art have also found a place — a very significant place — in our aesthetic culture. In the past they were classed as curios, by-products, decorative bric-à-brac. In our classical arts it was easy to distinguish an *objet d'art* from a work of art; this was not always so easy in Romanesque art; in Sumerian art it became quite impossible. The objects described in our art catalogues as *de haute curiosité* partake, almost always, of both qualities. Amongst the objects coming to us from cultures historically remote, it seems possible to distinguish those which apparently were not intended to rank beside the major works. Judged on these lines, a sacred figure of small dimensions would be regarded as an "object," while a non-religious figure of a certain size and scope would be a "work of art." Thus the mere "object" would qualify for an *objet d'art* owing to the presence of *style*.

But we know that outstanding works of any given art have more to them than their style; and that, while the creative act in art consists in the achievement of a new style in supersession of another, our aesthetic culture distinguishes (whether or not it uses the term "masterpieces" to describe them) works that, though linked up with their style, break through it as a butterfly breaks through its chrysalis. We also see that there is an obscure affinity between these works; an Egyptian statue, indeed a Sumerian, is promptly assigned to this class the moment it is exhumed; whereas the most virulent "ancestor" of the New Hebrides does not belong to it. Our terminology draws an excellent distinction between these two classes of work, describing the "ancestor" as a carving, and less readily as a statue.

Such terms as Negro art and Oceanian art persistently confuse the issues. Obviously there is no Negro art; there are African arts. If we rule out pre-history, we find a black

man's art following a *processus* that has become familiar to us; not only that of Benin and Ife (we do better not to call the latter "realistic"), but in a less degree that of the Bakuba tribe and the figures of Bushongo kings. Whatever be the material employed for this architectural and ornate stylization (which makes us think of a Byzantine art lacking its Christ), one feels that bronze is its true medium. While favouring kings as its subjects, this art also copes successfully with everyday themes, stylizing our sixteenth-century adventurers with a quite Caucasian brio. Then we have what are miscalled fetishes — masks and figures of ancestors: an art of a collective subjectivism, in which the artist builds up forms internally conceived yet recognizable by all, thus mastering with his art not that which is seen but what one does not see. On the one hand we have the ivories and bronzes of Benin, that kingdom in

JORUBAS. IVORY

which velvet was woven, and, on the other, the fabulous hunters of the rock-face paintings and all that art puts to their service; in that haunted dusk whence sally forth

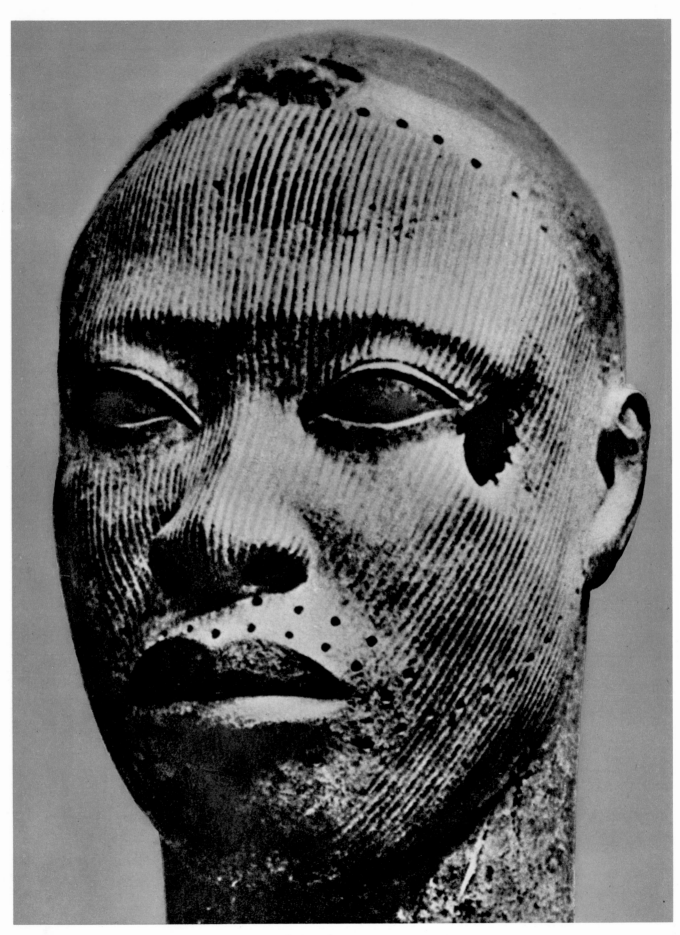

IFE (NIGERIA). BRONZE HEAD

BENIN.   ARCHER (BRONZE)

BASUTOLAND (S. AFRICA). ROCK-FACE PAINTING

the panther-men and antelope-men, we see the mask by means of which the sorcerer with his bird-skull necklet harks back to the age of Saturn.

Both these voices are known to Oceania, and a buckler from the Trobriands differs from a New Britain clay-moulded skull as it does from a woven New Guinea mask.

KOREDUGA. "VULTURE-MAN"

What is the link between a Congo mask and the pre-dynastic knife-handle of Gebel el Arak or the Sumerian figures of the third millenary before Christ? However steeped these are in the darkness of an underworld, or in that realm of blood whence rose the Aztec figures, they sponsor an attitude of men who challenge the universe — that attitude which founds kingdoms and builds cities.

Sumerian art belongs to a world of death; nevertheless it spread from Sumer to the Caucasus, after conquering Babylon. Remote in space and time, a Mayan figure may evoke a realm of forms of which we can make nothing, but not at all one of formlessness; and confronting the ageless faces hewn in granite or lava-rock, the carved prows of the Polynesian canoes dance like flotsam of a day. The supreme language of blood, like that of love, is the language of the temple. And, lacking temples, the nomads of the Mongolian steppes found their substitute in the Empire.

Thus we are beginning to see, in all the regions of the world our culture has recently annexed, an order, indeed a hierarchy; Benin art belongs to the historical arts,

PREDYNASTIC EGYPT. GEBEL EL ARAK

some of the Congo styles engender figures in which, no less than in Egyptian art, man is present. The striped masks of the Baluba tribe are further from *The Beggar Woman*, from that statue of an "ancestor" in the Antwerp Hessenhuis, than are these latter from certain Romanesque figures. By dint of being opened ever wider, the fan of savage arts is breaking up, and the striped mask seems as far from the almost Cingalese figures of Benin as are the carvings of Hopi Indians from Mayan bas-reliefs.

BALUBAS (BELGIAN CONGO). MASK

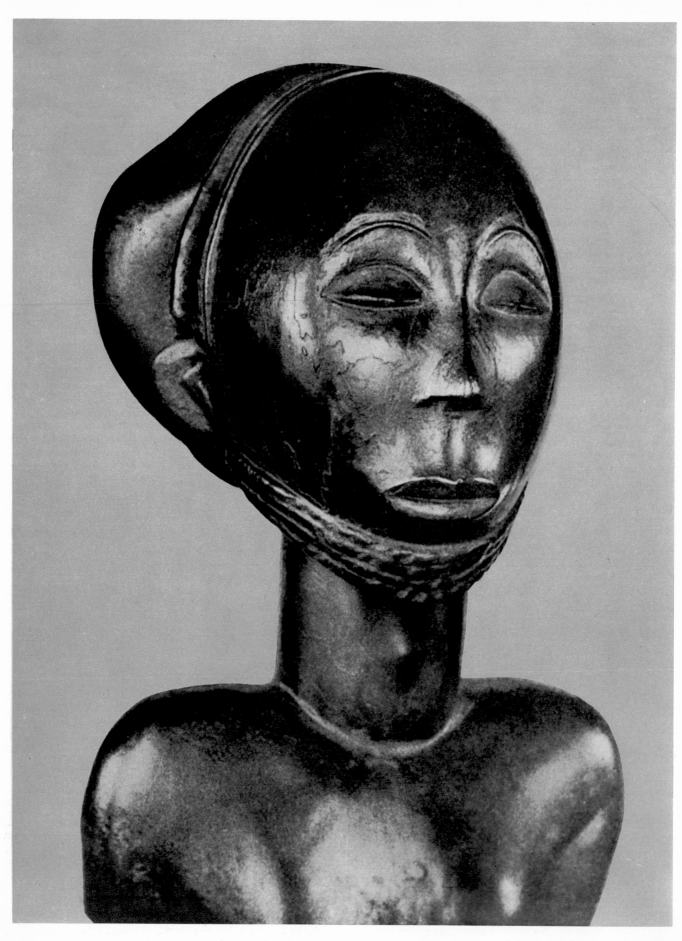

BALUBAS (BELGIAN CONGO).   ANCESTOR (HESSENHUIS)

BALUBAS (BELGIAN CONGO).   THE BEGGAR WOMAN

NEW GUINEA. ANCESTOR

There is an odd parallelism between the experience of the ideology which set out to justify Impressionism and that which claims to justify the forms of savage art. The former, sponsoring Monet, found itself confronted by Cézanne and Van Gogh; the latter, sponsoring the geometrical and often monochrome forms of the Congo, is confronted by the many-coloured trunks of the New Hebrides. A prolific harvest of discoveries, seconded by our enthusiasm, led us from African art to the Oceanian art nearest akin to it; then to arts at a short remove from it; and finally to arts whose forms are utterly unlike it. The arts of Oceania differ all the more from those of Africa because they have more colour: brown, angular, pre-Columbian looking figures in New Zealand; white, brown and red in New Ireland and the Bismarck Archipelago; parti-coloured in the New Hebrides. But these last belong to a quite different art; they are moulded, and have lost all trace of the "knife-blade" accent. They make good by their colour, sometimes subtle, sometimes strident, this stridency being due to violent contrasts of deep ultramarines, pinks and miniums, which our painters have not so far discovered (but they will). Applied to the dull, crackled clay, these give the bright, ornamental passages the vividness of pastels, and are utterly different from the architectural colour of other savage arts. (Here, too, the "rich" materials originally employed have been overlaid, as it were, by the dubious glamour of decomposition.) One step

more, and we arrive at the plumed Hawaiian helmet of the Musée de l'Homme, and Peruvian feather cloaks. What trace is here of Nigerian cubism, or of the tectonic planes of Senegambia? The vital difference between Polynesian art and African art is not that the former is in two dimensions (which indeed it not invariably is), but that it sets up against a build-up of volumes the elaborate formlessness of, for instance, the rush masks of the Sepik River; it is the only art to which this term applies. The modelling of the skulls overlaid with clay is not due to chance, any more than is the modelling of the ancestors of the New Hebrides, or the way in which the woven masks are plaited. But these shocks of hair worked in reeds, in feathers or vegetable fibre, and the spatulate noses, are not intended to build up a structural pattern. Incoherence, making its own laws and thereby imposing its authority, can sometimes have the driving force of Rimbaud's poetry; indeed the art of the New Hebrides parallels Rimbaud no less faithfully than Graeco-Buddhist art parallels Saint-John Perse; only, its shrillness and grotesqueness rasp our nerves, without penetrating to our culture. Despite their power (so much superior to that of the Sepik rush masks), the masks and ancestors of the New Hebrides are not statues, hardly sculpture at all; but oftener paintings, and always of specific objects.

"How can you like them and at the same time like Poussin and Michelangelo?" we may be asked simultaneously both by Poussin's champions and by defenders of the

SEPIK (NEW GUINEA). RUSH MASK

savage races, by Molière's bourgeois and the playboys of Montparnasse. Yet the attempts of the latter to whittle down the legacy of the ages to their by-products are as futile as the exaggerated rationalism of the former. While it is always interesting to ascertain our reasons for liking what we like, it is useless to argue what we "ought" to like. Art is the creation of the artist, not of the pundit, even though he be an artist too ; and I do not know a single great painter of to-day who does not respond (if in differing degrees) both to certain works of savages and to Poussin.

When the first mask reached Europe, what bond of kinship was there between Poussin and Grünewald, between Michelangelo and Chartres ? We must begin by noting that Poussin stands for something more than the "tapestry" of Rome and Versailles that his name conjures up for us, and that his imitators brought off as well as he ; we have in mind that subtle crystalline "Cézannian" quality to which his followers were blind, but which Cézanne so well recaptured. Grünewald's unrestrained emotionalism has a very different accent, but it too has its accent, and we cannot "understand" painting without understanding these accents, which resemble that element of poetry which it is impossible to put across in translation — and which is the essential stuff of poetry. Thus, if we disregard provisionally (as we may do for the "rational" elements of the poem) what painting has to tell us on its rational level, we find that the accents of the masters, even if they have no affinity between them — in the sense in which Poussin's, Corot's and Cézanne's accents are obviously akin — have nevertheless something in common, and our response to art is conditioned by the presence of that something, as our poetry is conditioned by the presence of that in it which could not conceivably be prose. It is the accent the *Housekeeper* would acquire were it to become a Braque, the Villeneuve *Pietà* were it to become a Cézanne, the Isenheim altar were it to become a Van Gogh.

In art, that word "accent" carries two meanings, and the relation between them is instructive. The "accents" of the painter (not to be confused with his "touches" or brushstrokes) are the means by which he *de*-composes the visible world; but he is not a great painter unless these are arranged so as to create *his* accent and are means to a coherent *re*-composition. Far from being eclectic and taking pleasure in a diversity of forms, our modern pluralism is based on our discovery of the elements that very diverse works of art have in common.

Those accents and that accent (as defined above), those dispersals and that plenitude, are present no less in the fetish, when it "comes off" as a work of art. They could become fully perceptible only when the Angel of Rheims had ceased to be an angel, and the *Thinker* to be an heroic figure. But in the case of the mask and the ancestor, neither is, for us, a magical or ancestral object, any more than a mediaeval Virgin is the Virgin. If painting has a language specific to itself, and is not a means of representation or suggestion, that language is present whatever the portrayal or suggestion — or even abstraction — with which it chances to be associated. And we credit a man who knows what Masaccio has in common with Cézanne and in what ways he diverges from him, with a truer understanding of Masaccio than that possessed by Quattrocento specialists to whom Cézanne means nothing.

It is not because our pluralism extends from classical art to Gothic, thence to Primitive and barbarian art, and finally to the art of savages — it is not because of this all-inclusiveness that our pluralism tenders a welcome to the fetish; but because no plastic expression is foreign to the language on which it is based. Thus we may fancy music, after being for many centuries yoked with words (the simple Philistine still thinks they should "go together," likewise painting and representation), being one day freed from them; and can we doubt that in that sudden dawn of freedom men would have discovered both its aptitude for invocation of the divine — the soaring splendours of a Beethoven — and the naïve charm of the rebeck crossed by the plaintive accents of the bagpipes? Now that painting's language has been "isolated" — painters have never failed to apprehend it, even when it was most involved in the extraneous — we can interpret the vast repertory of forms hostile to illusive realism, from old Bibles to grotesques. Provided we have art, not culture, in mind, the African mask and Poussin, the "ancestor" and Michelangelo, are seen to be not adversaries, but polarities.

For, once civilization had ceased being dominated by its gods, art emerged as a world of its own, existing in its own right, and the kinship of these "accents" became perceptible; and now it was viewed as a whole, art acquired, for a certain category of men, the power of remaking the scheme of things, setting up its brief eternity against man's yet briefer life. The will to hear the challenge or appeal addressed by a master-piece to other masterpieces, and then to all works qualified to hear it, is characteristic of every artist — and indeed of every true connoisseur; and likewise, the will to extend to new accents the overtones that each deep-sounding accent conjures up — from one Romanesque tympanum to another, from one Tuscan school to another, from one Mesopotamian style to another and, calling from archipelago to archipelago, the Oceanian figures.

A painter with little interest in music may admire, in a detached way, some great musical work, and sometimes grasp its import, but each encounter with a great work of plastic art is, for him, a very different experience. To be a musician does not mean casually to enjoy music, it means going out of one's way to hear it; and being a painter is not merely glancing at works of art. And thus it has always been, whether the artist's obsession centres on Roman antiquities dug up from the earth, on Chartres or on the Musée de l'Homme. The supreme power of art — and of love — is that they urge us to seek to exhaust, in them, the inexhaustible!

Our eagerness to absorb all is nothing new; what *is* new is that it leads to resus-citations whose message fascinates us no less when its values are hostile to us than when they are companionable.

For, though we are responsive both to the peculiar quality of the mask and to that of Poussin, they do not play the same part in our culture.

We have seen how, in Africa, the object or utensil tended to become the work of art in so far as the civilization was building up, from precedent to precedent, its history; in so far as it ceased doing so, the work of art reverted to the object. I do not say: "In so far as the civilization lapsed into savagery." The paintings of the Pygmies fail to impress us; indeed it well may be that total "savagery" has no art. Like the cannibal, the "gentle savage" of romance has left the scene. We know that the Tahitians were much less cruel than the Confucian sages who enacted so many brutal laws; for us civilization means not gentleness but self-awareness and human achievement.

That symbolic form, the romantic "savage" of our time, is neither good-natured nor fierce; he is a man possessed. Thus in the ritual dance of the Loyalty Islanders there comes a moment when the dancers suddenly make way for the young girls, who, painted in black and motionless as Egyptian figures, accompany their singing with rhythmic undulations of white flowers festooned between them; and here we have the selfsame surrender to the elemental powers as in the bloody rites of the New Hebrides. If an art utterly remote from ours, and endorsing the most hideous sacrifices, grips us, is this because of the glimpses it gives us of the chaos of man's beginnings, or not, rather, for what it expresses of man's ability to escape from chaos, even though no way of escape lies open to him, save through blood and darkness? So-called primitive civilizations are antithetic to civilized man — but likewise to the concept of "historical" man.

The confusion is intensified once the Ethnological Museum starts calling itself, as in France, the Musée de l'Homme, and takes a place in our culture, as an institute for both exploring and pushing back the frontiers of history — a form of history which very soon tends to join forces with biology. But if the pre-historian sets about his exploration on the same lines as the historian, what he comes on is something different from the stuff of history. For pre-history is not a vague, diffused form of history; it might better be called "anti-history," and the man of whom it gives us glimpses is, as is often the African or South Sea islander, anti-historic. This is why psychoanalysis finds itself so well at home here. And at least as much as in the cave-man, we are interested in the "folklore man," his next-of-kin, whose art seems sometimes to affiliate his figures to those of savage races, but also serves to define the creative processes and evolution of the latter.

Some Breton wooden crucifixes (not the wayside "calvaries") are, like the Nowy Targ *Christ,* Christian only in appearance. They pertain much less to some degenerate form of Christian art than to a vital impulse far older than Christianity, which has seeped into a Christian form after assuming many another. This is an art of the profoundly human, which clothes itself in the forms of successive periods of history, much as the moon's impartial light bathes men's successive palaces. True, there are also ruined palaces — hence the difficulty in defining where history ends, pre-history begins; but between the historical arts and these there is the same irreconcilable difference as between the epoch of the kingdoms and that of the cave-man.

The art of the European Retrogression was as foreign to the art of savages as was Greek art. Doubtless every culture in dissolution tends towards an art of this

THE NOWY TARG CHRIST (POLAND)

nature ; not because it sponsors nothingness, but because it expresses a mentality to which man has invariably harked back with every ebb-tide of a civilization. Its forms are the basic forms of the eternal return, and it is bound up with the cult of those anniversaries of the earth whose traces survive in our calendar, in our harvest festivals and rites of Spring.

The symbol of this civilization of all time is not the Nowy Targ *Christ* but the festival ; whereas that of the beginning of ours is the Pyramids. The Nowy Targ *Christ* and the Merovingian figures may be deemed impure because those who carved them had seen other portrayals of Christ ; likewise the makers of the peasant masks of Switzerland had, of course, seen churches.

The purity of that which lies not only outside history but outside Time usually finds expression in the impermanent ; thus, though the New Hebridean when he wishes to give the ancestors a voice carves them on hollowed-out tree-trunks made into tom-toms, he also carves them in a particularly perishable wood, that of the tree-fern, and covers them with spiders' webs. And in the wind of the immemorial the straw-men sway. . .

But it is not the straw-men we have revivified. We no longer necessarily assume that the man whose place lies outside history is a misfit, or a by-product; we see him as a different human type. We have an inkling that, while historical cultures have set

THE MOIS. STRAW-MAN

the trend of the arts that enter into art-history, the non-historical ages (proto-history, "unrecorded time") gave rise to more than buffalo-heads mounted on pikes or rags tied to trees on hillsides — they had their own *styles* as well: those, for instance, of the cave-men. Thus the mistaken theory that all savage art is the work of untrammelled instinct is losing ground, and we now are learning that style is not bound up with what we call civilization, or even with certain stages of culture.

Still we can see how easily that false assumption arose, at a time when history was identified with the path which led men from the Pelasgian huts to the Acropolis. Once history ceased being the record of our civilization alone, and that of our religion, it re-instated, behind Sumer and Memphis, as behind the earliest towns of Crete, India, China and Mexico, the shadowy hinterland which had been that of the pre-Hellenic world.

But paintings of the Magdalenian period have none of the anarchy of the formless. Indeed, now that we have come to admire the work of so-called Primitives, it has been but a step to the belief that style finds its strongest expression in forms that are foreign to the highest cultures. But this is really an optical illusion, bred of the mind and due to the fact that we are often as much impressed by the schematic lay-out of the seemingly naïve and elementary as by that of sophisticated art. Still there is more in it than that; it seems certain that the Altamira bison, the Castellón and Rhodesian hunters are, in fact, consciously elaborated works; as are the Scythian plaques, the prows of drakkars, and Armorican coins — and this is no less true of many African masks and ancestors and Oceanian figures.

ALTAMIRA.   SUPERIMPOSED ANIMALS

Though art keeps step with the march of history, an age that has no history does not necessarily express itself in a static art. Not all civilizations which seem unaffected by the lapse of time are unaffected by it in the same way.

The Middle Ages are not identical with Egypt; or very slow rhythms with immobility. Even in a culture steeped in the eternal a sculptured figure does not escape influences of its period; as in all ages, its first appearance is invested with an immediate appeal, which dwindles with the years. If it is created solely for some ceremonial purpose or, when burnt, replaced by another meant to be its replica, this process of dwindling operates more slowly, but no less surely. (In any case it is but seldom that races depicting living forms, depict them solely for ritual purposes.)

Even Byzantine art, in which the very calligraphy of the images was subject to inflexible rules, never quite achieved immobility.

Instinctive expression has no style; this is why the drawings of madmen and children have a calligraphy peculiar to themselves, but not a style; whereas the masks of savage races, which assert and body forth a specific conception of the world, have one. This conception can be expressed in more than one way and certain faculties of men may be transformed and enriched within a social order which to us seems static; else primitive religions would not have evolved — and Egyptian art would never have been born.

Thus even in a world seemingly unchanging, plastic forms are constantly being modified, improved on — as are the religious forms — and often under their influence. Even our wooden Romanesque Virgins, though the person represented was the same, differed considerably, and did not grow from faith, like apples growing from the same appletree. Even those who, with their cult of the so-called unconscious, showed the greatest enthusiasm for Negro art, really viewed it from the same angle as those who disdained it; what the former admired, the latter despised, in it was its approximation to the art of children.

But the affinity our age attributes to the works of savages, of children and of madmen, covers what are very different processes. Childish expression (this, anyhow, is truly instinctive) is a sort of monologue; the madman's is a dialogue whose sharer plays a passive part; whereas the savage's expression is not a monologue at all. His art invites the spectator's response, as did Romanesque and early Gothic. Much as Italian styles from the thirteenth to the sixteenth century came to portray the world of appearances in an ever more lifelike manner, even so some African styles seem gradually to have made theirs whatever links man up with the dark, invincible powers of an elemental world.

What is the African artist aiming at? Often he pays no heed to resemblance. Expression, yes — if we mean an expression as specific to itself as that of music, and

THE GABOON. PONGWE MASK

very different from such passionate expressions of the face as those of Japanese masks or the Graeco-Roman theatre. So different, indeed, that what, at a first glance, distinguishes an African mask from a European "folk" mask is precisely the specific expression of the former and the "expressionism" of the latter. African art has never aimed at suggesting anything by means of realism, even of a grotesque or feverishly emotive order (in

SWISS FOLK MASK (LÖTSCHENTAL)

which it fares quite badly), save when it aped foreign models. In cases where it trenches on the supernatural, it may be regarded as evocative of the unknown; but there are other cases (especially where figures of ancestors and animals are concerned) when, desisting from evocation, it concentrates on perfecting its mastery over forms, whether by ornamenting them with reproductions of tattoo-marks (as in the large Bakuba

IVORY COAST. MASK

figures), or by making them more complex (as in the polished masks of the Ivory Coast), or more architectural and coherent (as with certain ancestors of the Gaboon), or by stripping them down and (as in some Pongwe masks) scoring them with strongly indented linear patterns. In the making of these wooden effigies, though they lie only on the fringe of historic art, chance plays no more part than in the making of Benin bronzes, and, no less than these, they aspire to a quality apart from their efficacity as instruments of magic. Indeed it is common knowledge that aesthetic considerations bulk large in the works of certain Polynesian groups, by whom God is defined as "the source of harmony." Often, no doubt, Negroes are artists because they are men possessed; but sometimes, too, they are "possessed" because they are temperamentally artists.

Like the arts of the most civilized races, those of savages tend to create, alongside the real world, a world ruled by laws of their own making. African style is often more than stylization; but even when it is conditioned by the supernatural to the point of becoming an ecstatic geometry, we can trace (or, anyhow, guess) the lines on which it thus moved from strength to strength. The function of the spirit-antelope is to suggest the

THE GABOON.   ANCESTOR

SUDAN. MASK CREST : ANTELOPE

antelope, without being one; that is why Sudanese art diagrammatizes it. Its diagram might well be a mere sign. But from this sign the artist seeks to build up a form. The limbs of Europeanized fetishes look like limbs; those of the best effigies of ancestors *signify* limbs but do not resemble them; they are "interpreted." The genius of the black sculptor leads him to adjust all his forms to the unity of a style; as do our sculptors. Poussin "embellishes" each arm in terms of his picture as a whole, just as the Negro schematizes or even invents an arm so as to give his sculpture an indefeasible unity. Both expel from their work all that does not belong to it, and the script of the Pongwe mask (which brings Klee to mind) links up with the fiercest Dogon figures, the most architectural Guinea ancestor, the most angular Sepik ancestor (and, perhaps too, with the most lyrical colour-patches of the New Hebrides), by virtue of the presence of a controlling personality. And from Benin to Polynesia, by way of thousands of half-fledged figures, we respond to all that this commanding presence sometimes wrests triumphantly from a mere effigy in straw.

The attention bestowed on African art by our artists, when first it invaded the European scene, was

SUDAN. DOGONS. THE MALE AND FEMALE PRINCIPLES

directed less to individual works than to a style they symbolized collectively, a style that pitted new values (with a quite unprecedented truculence) against the academic values. The Gothic artists had made a similar incursion — but with this difference that our art museums hastened to "filter" them, and that, anyhow, the cathedrals could easily be seen. (It is well worth comparing, in this context, the galleries of great mediaeval German painting, with those of provincial museums, even the Bavarian Museum.) Now that the shock of that first contact is beginning to wear off, we limit our attention to the masterpieces of savage art; but our modern sensibility does not pick out one mask in the *ensemble* in the same way as it set up *all* the masks, collectively, against Bonnat.

The *Kings* of Chartres are no longer seen by us as barbaric expressions of stupendous power, but as expressions of the Christian genius. When we talk of a masterpiece of the Congo, we speak of a Congo figure but also of a masterpiece; this figure belongs to savage art, yet has its own civilization implicit in itself. Nor do we always regard as outstanding works those which have an obscure kinship with our own art, as has *The Beggar Woman*. The effigies of the New Hebrides which we prefer owe nothing to us — and we make no doubt of preferring them. For though, at the extreme of savagery, that mask with fishes' teeth and that ancestor whose bones show through his body are utterly alien to us, *they are not alien to our art*, and under their auspices their myth is undergoing a transformation.

"Primitive" forms impress us, to begin with, by their huge proliferation, but we reserve our lasting interest for a select few; and those our selection brings together are other than the "lucky flukes." That company of the dispossessed loses by being viewed *en masse*. Thus, after surveying a hundred New Ireland effigies, we prefer to isolate two or three and toy with the illusion that they are the work of a single imaginary sculptor (not wholly of his time and a little of ours) who may take his place beside some others bearing the names of Gaboon, Congo, Haida, Sepik and so forth. Already in some instances we are beginning to substitute the concept of the individual sculptor for that of a collective style; thus we know some ten other works by the maker of *The Beggar Woman*. (An exceptional case, perhaps; still the process of elaboration of the styles of savages, though more collective and slower than that of ours, is no longer unfamiliar.) But though his most significant works may give us, like our modern masterpieces, the feeling of a triumph of the creative mind, the fact remains that, in any ethnological museum, we also have a feeling of witnessing some carnival of art emerging from a mythical past — of an art in which man is dispossessed in favour of some queer, shadowy, pre-human dream.

If artists gifted with a sense of colour as exacerbated as that of the sculptors of the New Hebrides fail to compose painted scenes, this is because no setting can be conceived

NEW IRELAND FIGURES

of in which their painted effigies would seem at home, as do Hieronymus Bosch's devils in his ghoulish landscapes. The proper *rendez-vous* of savage masks is surely a witches' Sabbath or a primaeval paradise, not in any scene thought up by a painter; linked up as they are with fertility or funeral rites, and murmurous with long-forgotten voices, these effigies strike us as necessarily isolated figures. Unless art comes to their rescue, they are no more than "objects," *data* of short-lived schools.

Fashion and the theatre, likewise, dabble in the intense or muted colour of the masks and ancestors of the New Hebrides, in which, when a horde of them are brought together in a museum, we seem to see a *haute couture* of Death. These glittering ghosts really belong to poetry — which is why Surrealism has taken them to its bosom. But Surrealism does not propose to further culture; it rejects it, in favour of the dream.

Whereas our culture does not set out to reject the dream, but to incorporate it. Our Middle Ages, too, gave intimations of what the festival bequeathed from pre-history may have been; but once his Carnival was over, mediaeval man fell to building cathedrals, and his rulers had not "ancestors," but forbears.

Our troubled epoch seeks to discern in the art of savages not only the expression of another world, but also that of those monsters of the sea-depths which psycho-analysis fishes for with subtle nets — and politics or war, with dynamite. Like the Chinese or the "noble savage" of the eighteenth century, our Primitives step forth obligingly, when called from their retreats. But J. J. Rousseau had not the slightest wish to become a Tahitian, or Diderot a Chinese, or Montesquieu a Persian; they merely wished to annex the wonders and the wisdom of these exotic creations of their fancy, and invited them to arraign "civilization," not with a view to destroying, but to perfecting it.

We must not lightly dismiss these messengers who brought us so many things (including the Revolution); but our immediate concern is with the message brought by their successors. The dark forebodings they convey are not more compelling in so far as European civilization is threatened (to begin with, by itself), than in so far as Western civilization is still the victor. For even if their advent heralded the beginning of a death-agony, it would also signify the last lap of a conquest; the jazz-dancing American soldiers are not yet converted to voodooism. In that obscure hinterland we lose our way so easily that we confuse African effigies made for sacrificial rites with those which were made for festivals, the spirit of blood with the wheat-spirit, tutelary ancestors with ghosts.

The tantrist art of Tibet, which is directed in a much more obvious way towards the Powers of the underworld, leaves us indifferent. Its painting is an academicized form of Bengalese art, steeped in conventions (as are, if on other lines, Ming art and traditional Russian art). Its masks aim at conveying an exceptionally potent suggestion of the other world, but they are used in stage performances; indeed the ageless religious ballet of the East is but a stage show — whereas the black men are "possessed" by their ceremonial rites. Hence the affiliation between Tibetan masks and the theatre; they stylize facial expressions — anger, cruelty and so forth — and their searching for theatrical effect is enough to disqualify them from being an "art." Whereas African effigies are not cumbered with anecdotes of a netherworld . . .

Thus it is the quality of their specific expression that grips us in works coming to us from the primaeval depths. Our admiration of Aztec figures (soaked as they are in blood) is not proportioned to the number of skulls bedecking them. India has

known for untold ages the pomp of sexual and funeral rites, and the bas-relief of the *Kiss* at Ellora, and the Dances of Death, rise from a richer darkness than the Taras of Tibetan banners. But the Dance of Death has a cosmic significance for us only by reason of its specific accent, and once it loses this, becomes as vapid as any Jesuit "saint." Lacking this accent, the work of art is dumb. And, finally, the Dance of Siva, while responsive to the voices of the abyss, incorporates them in the world of men ; so completely, indeed, that those who know little of Hinduism, totally fail to perceive that the god is trampling down a dwarf and to recognize

TIBETAN MASK (BEGINNING XIXth CENT. ?)

in him a symbol of death and resurrection. Now, every work of art that imparts a sense of aesthetic quality links up the netherworld that it expresses with the world of day ; and every work that moves us thus testifies to the triumphant element in man — even though he be a man in ecstasy. And at last we are becoming qualified to judge if these voices of the abyss have any value other than that of stablishing in man a more compelling awareness of his manhood.

However debatable may be the hierarchy of works of art, in an age which declines to base their precedence either on the most human or on the least human manner of expression, none of us places on the same level a Chartres *King* and even the most attractive of scarecrows, nor yet that same *King* and a Romanesque statue chosen at random. We seem chary of dispelling the shadows that enwrap our treasure-house of the Past, yet that treasure-house has not ceased existing ; indeed we may see in the great San Francisco Exhibition to which each country was asked to contribute a single picture, the latest token of its permanence.

Our age has discovered that the great Buddhist, Egyptian and Gothic works of art can rank beside Giotto and Rembrandt in our admiration. And it expects to discover yet other works which, while not relaying these latter as obviously as Rembrandt takes over the torch from Michelangelo, will perhaps be as different from these as they are from one another.

The concept of art has become an open question; it is no longer pre-determinable. We know that, while a work of art is a response, and admired as such, it also so happens — during the periods when great changes are coming over art — that, instead of answering, it silences problems which had hitherto been taken for granted. All the more because the kinship of forms (compendious enough to suggest the presence, still perhaps latent, of an order similar to the predetermined orders of the past), now that these forms are seen to undergo a metamorphosis, comes up against a paradoxical discovery — that the basic continuity of art can be ensured only by striking out in new directions.

Art has thus become a field in which all works that move us are affiliated. It did not "spread" from Greece to Oceania; rather, a new notion of art has arisen, which will perhaps be submerged, but not destroyed, by one still vaster. "Beauty" is a case in point; it has become for us merely one province of art's kingdom. The only change is that the choice of works that constitute our treasury has ceased, for the moment, to be "rationalizable."

The idea we have of the masterpiece is apt to be distorted by that of the perfect work: an idea that leads to much confusion once we apply it to works by artists other than those whose supreme value it expresses. Thus, while Raphael's art was guided by that ideal of perfection, Grünewald's obviously was not, and perhaps the craving for perfection does most to shape an art which deems itself subordinate to some illustrious precedent; Poussin was, evidently, more obsessed with this ideal than was Pheidias. Many periods have rated highly this quality, but not all detected it in the same works. Thus nowadays perfection of colour has taken the lead of perfect drawing; it has even been possible to exclude the human figure. During the two centuries following his death, Chardin's art suffered a hundred years' eclipse; perhaps, before his eminence could be made good, it was needful that French painting should move on from Corot to Braque.

For us, perfection has ceased to be appraised in terms of an absolute; it is gauged in relation to ourselves. Each great art unearths or regains its perfection, just as it retrieves its ancestors; but a perfection of its own and not always the same as that of its forerunners.

Never has the artist appraised the masterpiece on the same lines as the aesthetician. During certain periods he saw in experiments a means of testing his abilities, with a view to the ultimate creation of a *magnum opus*, in which he hoped to embody all he thus had learned from these preliminary "exercises," and which, if it "came off," would equate the masterpiece of his dream; and this method of approach is still familiar to our architects. In most cultures this *magnum opus* meant the expression of the highest values. It is unlikely that the master of the Royal Portal of Chartres felt himself supremely committed in the shaping of a capital; that Pheidias set a higher value on the metopes of the Parthenon than on his statue of Athene. Or even that Michelangelo preferred the Uffizi *Holy Family* to the Medici Chapel or to the Sistine ceiling. Rembrandt, whose art obeyed no orders but its own, was "mobilized," so to speak, by *The Three Crosses* as Pheidias was by *Athene* and Grünewald by the Isenheim altar. Thus, too, Goya by the *Shootings of May 3*.

Perhaps we have here an origin of the misapprehension as to the part played by the "lofty theme." In such themes, indeed, genius found its most favoured medium of expression; they fired the artist with the most urgent desire to paint. And when faith was no longer the only factor, symbols and dead gods replaced living gods; a *Venus* by Titian, Poussin's Bacchanalia, expressed, in their eyes, values that could be partially substituted for religious values. But then painting, *per se*, became the supreme value and the note, echoing through the ages, that Rembrandt struck when he achieved a world worthy of Christ, was struck again by Vermeer and Chardin, when they built up a world worthy of the art of painting; and it is in such cases that the "exercise" and the major work, expressing the highest values of their age, seem to merge with each other.

And that chance seems to replace deliberation; but a form of chance that is not so much accidental as a gift of the gods. The hierarchy imposed by Cézanne on his canvases was based on that *realization,* "which," he said, "he brought off so rarely, and which the Venetians had so often achieved." Obviously by this word he did not mean effects of illusion, or emotional expression; nor did he mean the impossibility of enriching the picture with the imagination (in the sense given the word in the XVIth century). Those little gaps on the canvas which always worried him were unnoticed by most, and could have been filled by him alone. His soul-searchings as to the "realization" of a picture, not that of a scene, were due above all to the exercise of a power of whose precariousness he was only too well aware. And this power was what had replaced (from Rembrandt onwards) that which the Italians, and most Primitives, thought to be a matter of acquired and ordered knowledge... The artist has become a gambler, whose lucky *coup* is — the masterpiece.

But since the painter does not reproduce nature; since the game is played less between the landscape and his canvas than between the painting and himself; since there is a steady progress, if sometimes unapparent, from his first to his last picture; and since his task is to transform — his field of action is limited, to say the least, by the trend he gives this transformation and by the hold it gives him on things seen. The Villeneuve *Pietà,* the *Burial of Count Orgaz,* the *Three Crosses,* like the *Château noir,* do not aim at perfection— yet they are not mere lucky flukes. Clearly the painter has won — but what is it he has won?

To begin with, plenitude — which means no more necessarily rich texture or brilliant effects than construction or purity; nor does it mean tradition rather than innocent simplicity. What gives a great artist his immortality (whether he thinks he is serving beauty or God, his personality or painting) is that part of his work in which his art attains the greatest *density* — whether this art expresses itself in the tenuous vapours of Sung painting or the massive colour of a Rembrandt. Because in the struggle between the artist and the world, he achieves his independence, his victory, by the *deepening* of his resources. This victory bears the name of "mastery," even if all that vouches for it, after the glittering pageantry of the *Kermesse,* is the pale sheen of *Helena Fourment's Children.*

So persistent a legend has been built up round the great religious arts that the mere mention of their names conjures up before us, as it were, the devout farrago of some Breton "Calvary" — which is due no doubt to the extreme profusion of our cathedrals and of the Indian temples. Yet, once we are in the presence of a masterpiece, no mistake is possible; the Vézelay *Christ,* the Chartres *David,* the *Beau Dieu* of Amiens, *Uta,* the Wei Bodhisattvas, *Didufri,* even the best pre-Columbian and the Lagash statues are not less dominated by the master-minds that conceived them than are a Greek archaic figure, a Raphael, a Vermeer, a Chardin — indeed, the most "composed" picture. (Often when this domination affects only a portion of the work, some happy fracture makes good the masterpiece, by reducing the statue to its most dominated part.) Though all deeply felt faith involves the artist's surrender to it, his self-effacement as an individual does not imply that his art is similarly kept under; in the great religious arts, the artists' refashioning of the world in terms of their gods operates through themselves, just as the individualist artist remoulds the scheme of things in terms of painting. In the arts of magic, the limits of instinctive expression are set by local styles; the black sculptor regards as the "best" mask that which does its work best. And what chiefly implements its efficacity is the plenitude of its style. That Negroes can often name their great mask-makers; that nearly all the modelled skulls of the New Hebrides come from one little island (Toman); that in Africa, only sculptors whose talent was conspicuous were allowed to make the royal effigies that have come down to us — all these facts show that the status of the art of savages (always, in fact, linked up with the dance) resembles that of *cante jondo* with regard to music, and the psalm *vis-à-vis* poetry. Nevertheless psalms and the *cante jondo,* while neither odes nor operatic arias, are far from being mere vociferations.

Romanticism (even in its contemporary forms) has done much to merge the magician with the "possessed" man in the artist. When he staked his greatness on the answers man still gave the gods receding from the world, even though his voice echoed on the void, the teeming denizens of the underworld of consciousness began to rear their heads. We have seen how, in Goya as in Goethe, Nerval and Baudelaire, witches often served as midwives to the new art. And there now emerged a curiously persistent affinity between the obscure side of certain great works of art — not necessarily their "night side" — and the dark places of man's heart. (On which theme psychoanalysis — at last legitimately — may find much to say.) *The Shootings of May 3* is not superior to *The Charge of the Mamelukes* because it is better painted, but because immanent in it is a vision of Spain, of martyrdom, and something of that enigmatic glow which lurks in the misted gaze of Goya's "monsters." These intimations of the elemental were nothing new in art. The wings of the *Victory of Samothrace* do not merely uphold its triumphant line ; they had been the wings of the Egyptian sphinxes and were, later, to become those of angels. The loss of the head of Niké is regrettable, no more than that ; but the loss of her wings would have been the end of her.

While the expression, however indirect, of emotions stemming from archaic man adds a special *timbre* to the masterpiece, this invocation of the powers beneath the threshold is always at the service of what may be called its royal accent ; no monstrous form figures in art as an end in itself. I have already spoken of the reappearance of the devil, the return to dualism, which characterizes our age. But the language that the devil has forced us to listen to, is not solely that of savagery. For it summons up also, as we shall see, the only language against which the devil's is unable to prevail. The artist could adopt the methods of the arts of magic only by total self-surrender ; though that surrender might have a fascination for him *as a man,* he could not fail, *as an artist,* to be no less fascinated by the mastery revealed in works of art expressing the unknown. Need I repeat that a picture by a madman is not a Van Gogh, and that, in order to get some "extravagant" work into its just perspective, we need only bring it into line with similar works made by the same man ? Seared though it be by the undying fires erupting from the underworld, every masterpiece sponsors the progress of man's dominance. Whether it allies him with his gods or arrays him against them ; and whether it is to the gods of Babylon, to Christ, or to painting, that it dedicates him. It is on this plane — on which are mingled a feeling of man's deliverance and a feeling of the mastery inherent in the work of art — that our admiration of Vermeer and Chardin makes common cause with our admiration of the men who carved the Yun Kang rock-face, and our cathedrals, of Michelangelo and Rembrandt. Nothing can overcome the vigilance, like a deep-sea diver's, of the man of genius; no "dispossession" ruled out Goya's retouches or Rimbaud's erasures. The maker of masks may be "possessed" by demons, but by the same token he bends them to his creative will; the face of a Javanese Siva bespeaks a victory over the death's-head above it, and, though the Chartres sculptor was certainly "possessed" by Christ, it was not Christ who carved the Royal Portal.

SIVA. JAVA (IXth CENT.)

IV Not every day, nor even in every century, does a type of man emerge who, breaking off his immemorial relations with the cosmos, conquers the world anew. It was not at the bidding of the spirit of Macedonia that the Hellenistic spirit fell on a decline; nor at the behest of the Roman spirit that what remains of Rome is but a Coliseum and some churches spangled with mosaics amongst the brambles; but it is on the authority of the spirit of Europe, and owing to her discoveries, that Asia to-day is rejecting European domination. After disinterring three thousand years of history, Europe now dreams of conquering the entire past, a conquest never yet achieved; some epochs, indeed, could hardly retrieve their own immediate past. What, indeed, has this all-including rediscovery in common with the archaizing taste of, for instance, the Alexandrians? We are familiar with the archaism of certain ancient cultures (and the Chinese); it resembles the penchant of our Empire style for Egypt, and that of the nineteenth century for Gothic forms. But, amongst us, it is not the admirers of Rheims who admire pseudo-Gothic architecture; it is, rather, those who do not really care for Rheims. Our resemblances with Alexandria are of the slightest in this modern world which, within a mere hundred years, has been stripped of the dreams it had nursed since the era of the cave-men.

Those masks and ancestors we admire are being made no longer, and while in our museums they set us dreaming, the vulgarest manifestations of our own art are by way of killing them off in Africa; piously we recall the frescos of burnt-out Nara, while modern Japanese artists in third-rate towns are imitating Montparnassian painters whose "fame" does not even extend to Lyons. We photograph Ajanta, but the painters of the Calcutta school are Pre-Raphaelites; and the (much superior) art of the modern Mexicans has obvious affinities with ours. It is high time for us to perceive that, for three hundred years, the world has not produced a single work of art comparable with the supreme works of the West. What is challenged in our culture is challenged invariably by the past of other cultures; it is as if the all-conquering but chaotic culture that is ours were trying to destroy its humanistic heritage solely with the object of making good a worldwide humanism, and annexing, to this end, both what is apparently nearest its own art and that which is most profoundly foreign to it.

During the period following the first World War savage arts were hailed as allies of modern art — but allies against what? Neither Cézanne nor Renoir disdained Titian, and Manet venerated Frans Hals. Some artists and aestheticians still maintain that modern art is diametrically opposed to certain specified earlier arts; whereas the public reconciles them quite easily, enjoying both alike; indeed the enthusiasm it displays for modern painting leads it to crowd the Louvre, not to desert it. It was not the museum as such that was assailed, but the "lesson" it was supposed to convey. Whether our modern artists asserted that Manet was "as good as" Rembrandt, or not so good, what they looked for was what Rembrandt has in common with Manet. And they discovered that he stood for nothing hostile to their art, for a would-be Rembrandt is not an echo of Rembrandt, but an echo of the void, and a new Rembrandt would have no more likeness to the real Rembrandt, than the latter has to the Villeneuve *Pietà,* or Piero della Francesca has to the *Koré of Euthydikos.*

A greater exponent of magnificence, Michelangelo is a less great colourist than Vermeer; to blame him for not being Vermeer (as El Greco once blamed him for not being Titian) is as futile as blaming Vermeer for not being Michelangelo — and would it be less futile blaming Braque or Matisse for this? If the various epigones of Rembrandt and Michelangelo's plagiarists exasperate us, this may be because Michelangelo's presence, and Rembrandt's, not only in our art galleries but also in our hearts, affects us more intensely than it affected the men of an age when their imitators were admired. Never do the organ-notes of Michelangelo's supreme works reverberate more amply than when they are confronted by some New-Hebridean figure or by a Dogon work; thus, too, a lamp shines brightest in the heart of darkness.

The return to favour of barbaric arts was only a single, relatively superficial aspect of the great change undergone by the art heritage of Europe as a whole. When beauty ceased being the criterion of art, not only the fetishes but a vast assemblage of forgotten treasures, a reflux of the past, was brought back on the rising tide. Delacroix would not recognize "his" Rubens; nor Fromentin (who, though no Delacroix, was also no fool), "his" Rembrandt; indeed no Greek Master, "his" museum. And the affinity we seem to discern between our reconstitutions of the past and modern art is all the more baffling now that we are beginning to suspect that, while knowing much about the forms, we know but little of the spirit of our art.

It is not easy to find the common measure of an Impressionist landscape, a Van Gogh portrait, a Cézanne figure and a Maillol work of sculpture; and a survey of our contemporaries from Picasso to Dufy, by way of Rouault, Utrillo and Léger, reveals a diversity no less pronounced. But it is above all if we have failed to rid ourselves of the notion that the function of plastic art is representational, that we are baffled by this diversity; once this illusion is dispelled, we find that Sisley, who painted landscapes not as they look to the average man but as the painter *wished* to see them (i. e. subordinated to the picture), is not really so far removed from Braque who paints a still life as he *wishes* to paint it. A naked woman painted by Degas was "a nude," not a naked woman; and, above all, a picture. Though light was no more than one of the justifications claimed by the Impressionists for the use of pure colour "straight from the tube" (for a Monet, while more variegated as to colour and often sunnier than a Rembrandt, is not more luminous), this new art, after ceasing to serve representation, was not constrained to serve abstraction. True, it sometimes tended towards the abstract, because

it aimed at making good its conquest of a new world in terms of the artist's sensibility, not at expressing the unconscious or at purely architectural interpretation. Utrillo has often shown us, not better but more clearly than Corot, how effectively a landscape in which literal resemblance is ignored can be charged with sensibility. In any case an abstract work of art is the abstract expression of *something,* not the expression of an abstraction. In Degas' intensest pastels there is no more than a hint of the real — as in so many works of art from the days of Manet to those of Seurat, and in all the work of our contemporaries. The dramatic "fixation" of one element of the visible — of light with Monet, movement with Degas, volume with Cézanne — was a

CÉZANNE. LES DEUX PROMENEUSES

means, not an end ; but its end was not merely an individualization of the world ; their art did not aim at intensifying the real, but at disintegrating it — and re-integrating it into something other than itself. When we visit an exhibition of our modern pictures in Russia, in an Islamic country, or in Asia, what particularly strikes us in this ambience is their way of breaking up — with almost angry violence — living forms, at the behest of a "value" foreign to them.

This refusal to be ruled by appearance — in virtue of which modern art makes common cause with almost all it has resuscitated, is clearly not the outcome of any special manner of portrayal. What is being queried once again is the *value* of the world of appearances. The great arts of the past portrayed that which they held to be the most important, and employed this for the expression of their highest values. We have seen how in Greece, and again in the thirteenth century, appearance crept into art, at the same time as the human element permeated the divine. When any ancient art rejects appearance, its object (like that of ordinary idealization) is to endow the thing seen with a special quality ; as, for example, Byzantine art invested the world with holiness. But the Byzantines knew what they were after ; whereas our modern art, when it wrests its portrayals from the world of appearances, can hardly tell what end it serves thereby.

That it is engaged in a passionate attempt to enable individual man to master and annex the world around him is plain to see; and it is no less obvious that this activity of *transformation* is inherent in our culture, which aims far more at transfiguring the world than at adapting itself to its environment or accepting certain chosen elements of it. Science, in substituting its own world for the world of appearances, has pointed the way; but we know how alien science is to our art. Nor can we forget that our annexation, voracious though it be, is mindful not to assimilate *all* into itself; our modern style has summoned back to life certain religious modalities of art and those painters for whom painting was an absolute value, but it eschews such secular arts as those of ancient Rome, the lesser Dutch masters and the English portrait-painters, all of whom nineteenth-century official art took to its bosom. But neither Confucian China (T'ang art, yes, but not Ming art), nor Mogul India. Dare we assert that the value of a Gainsborough portrait, *qua* picture, of a scene by Mieris or one by an early Ming painter is lower than that of a second-rate Romanesque fresco? We are apt to read into the modern quest of tectonic form, often of effects of stridency, a deeper meaning, the quest of an *arcanum*. Akin to all styles that express the transcendental and alien to all others, our style seems to pertain to some religion of which it is unaware. Yet it owes its kinship with the former not to the expression of any transcendental world; rather, to its negation: indeed it seems like a photographic negative of the styles of the transcendent.

Needless to say, no style has ever been completely at the service of appearance, for reasons we have already given; still it is a far cry from Titian's Venice to Byzantium. Obviously the discrepancy between arts of the transcendent and the great religious arts is not due to the presence of Christ, or even that of God. Venice was no less Christian than Byzantium; but she was Christian in a different way. When we wonder what rival ideal can be set up against the ideal of beauty, as the great Venetians conceived it, what comes to our mind is not ugliness (always a relative concept), nor characterization, but — mystery. Whereas Greek culture sponsored man's right to stand up to his gods and arraign the universe, other cultures, no less whole-heartedly, brought man to judgment, invoking the authority of the eternal, or, more simply, all that is other than he. Neither death's certainty nor the dark lures of the underworld, nor the menaces of the fate-fraught stars have in all times prevailed against that soaring hope which has enabled human aspiration, winged with love, to confront the throbbing vastness of the nebulae with the puny yet indomitable forms of Galilean fishermen or shepherds of Arcadia. Strange indeed is that choice which the past seems to demand of us here and now — a choice whose making in other ages called for centuries of groping in the dark. On the one hand are the forms of all that pertains essentially to the human, from the beauty of women to the fellowship of men, from Titian's *Venus* to his *Pietà*. On the other hand are all those forms pertaining to the outside world, or man himself, which crush or baffle him, from Sphinx to fetish. The open hands of him who kneels in gratitude, and the arms clamped tightly to the body of the oriental, prostrate in obeisance — how many gestures, varying with the ages, are those of man communing with the sacrosanct!

But each form of the sacrosanct was regarded by those belonging to the civilization that gave rise to it, as a delineation of the truth; thus, for Byzantine men, the majesty of the Byzantine style was not the expression of a mere hypothesis. To us, however, these forms appeal only as forms — in other words, as they would be, were they the work of a contemporary (and, since actually this is unthinkable, they affect us in a very perplexing way) — or else as an expression of grandiose, mysterious visions, emanations of the sacrosanct. Thus we look at them from outside and rob them of that which was their very essence; for a religious civilization which took what it revered for a mere hypothesis is inconceivable.

Now the forms of all religious arts that have lost for us their sanctity have this in common (and it is no accident, but inherent in their very nature) that they differ from the "real." The style of a sacred art is, amongst other things, a technique for creating figures that, anyhow partially, escape from the thrall of the human. In fact we cannot conceive of a sacred art subservient to appearance. And what links up our modern art with the sacred arts is not at all that, like them, it has a transcendental significance, but that, like them, it sponsors only such forms as are discrepant from appearance.

From Sumerian to Negro art, from the art of the pre-Columbians to that of the Steppes, all forms which give us the impression of tending towards a "dispossession" of man are nourished by a disdain of appearance. What differentiates Titian from a fetish and even from Matisse is the fact that Titian was trying to adapt the visible world and painting to man, whereas the fetish aims at adapting man to the unknown, and Matisse at adapting him to painting. This is why Impressionism failed to deflect the course of modern art. Every form of expression of men and things, which the painter has accepted, indeed chosen, as the medium of his art, derives from the first smile of Greece or China, and is bound up with man, "possessed" by him — as is Goethe's "characteristic" and the caricature. Even this latter, though the antithesis of idealization, is less opposed to it than to the discrepant which, in its disdain of appearance, deals not in caricatures but in monsters. Technique apart, Expressionism has nothing in common with Impressionism; drama calls for more drastic values than a subtle volatilization of form. An arraignment, if it is to take effect, tends to set up against the scheme of things which it arraigns, a transcendent vision — that is to say, in art, a style

ST LUKE, PHOCIS.   ANASTASIS (MOSAIC, EARLY XIth CENT.)

intentionally discrepant from these things.   From Van Gogh to Rouault, by way of the
Flemish and Germanic Expressionists, the will to expression has been tempered by
the will to style; as it was, clumsily, at Byzantium, from Saint Luke's in Phocis to
Daphni, and has been, since then, more significantly.   We need but compare Daumier's
lawyers and judges to the dramatic, then supremely tragic, judges Rouault has
shown us.

DAPHNI. ANASTASIS (MOSAIC, END XIth CENT.)

DAUMIER. LAWYERS CONVERSING

The style of what I have named the discrepant is no more limited to the effects of an exceptionally dynamic expression of the individual than to those of an exceptionally keen vision. Painters themselves may have been misled in this respect; not so their pictures. Our style is the outcome of a will to the discrepant, dimly felt at first, then fully conscious. Like that of the Eastern Church, it is based on a conviction that the only world with which the artist is concerned is distinct from the world of appearance, which it does not so much express as parallel. An ikon does not profess to give us Christ's true likeness, but to furnish a compelling symbol of it; and our art is the creation of a world foreign to the real, not its expression.

The arts of "beauty" offer us scenes which, did they become real, would charm us; whereas the characteristic of an other-worldly art is that its figures could not conceivably revert to the human. Still the train of thought which leads the modern artist to paint forms discrepant from the real is, actually, not very different from that which led Renaissance painters to dedicate their art to beauty.

But our art does not express any single overriding value, as the Byzantine mosaics expressed the majesty of God. It is not, nor does it aspire to be, the expression of

ROUAULT. THE JUDGES (1937)

any ruling sentiment common to all in a culture based on this sentiment; the reason being that our age, so quick to admire that which it fails to understand, prefers on this account forms discrepant from reality, and whose meaning it cannot grasp. True, Byzantine artists did not see passers-by like ikons, any more than Braque sees fruit-bowls in fragments; nevertheless Braque's forms do not mean to twentieth-century France what the forms of Daphni meant to Macedonian Byzantium.

Yet after all, perhaps, Braque's attitude towards his forms is not so very different from that of the mosaic-makers towards those of their Christs, their prophets and their saints. . .

When the tumult and the shouting had died, and the man-in-revolt arisen upon the ruins of the French Revolution — when the art that the victorious *bourgeoisie* had called into being was an art of the imagination that repudiated all its works and ways (what was there in common between the *bourgeoisie* and Delacroix' *Crusaders*, or even Couture's *Caesar*, even Cormon's *Cain*?) — there co-existed for the first time not two schools, but two distinct functions of art. Historians of the future, if one day our works of art survive as memorials of a Europe blasted out of recognition and unremembered, will be led to assume that between 1870 and 1914 two antagonistic civilizations, in water-tight compartments, confronted each other. The art of the Steppes is as different from Chinese Han art, Byzantine art from Giotto's, as is the Luxembourg Museum from the Museum of Modern Art of to-day; as was the art-world of Bonnat, Cormon, Bouguereau and Roll from that of Manet, Seurat, Van Gogh and Cézanne. And this antagonism had nothing to do with any traditional "conditioning"; often as not the Independents had been trained in the same studios as their adversaries. Though these artists (whose prevailing attitude towards politics was one of scornful detachment) were hostile to middle-class values, they had no illusions about the proletariat who, on the rare occasions when they lingered before a picture-dealer's window, much preferred Bonnat to Degas. Here our sociologists should walk warily: the art which followed that bought formerly by the aristocrats, was not an art patronized by the middle class — it was an art that *nobody* bought.

The "outcast" artist was coming on the scene. And haunted by visions of *his own* absolute, confronted by a culture growing more and more unstable, the painter was led to find in his very ostracism the source of an unprecedented fertility. After having traced on canvas, like wavering blood-streaks, the records of so many starveling pilgrimages, the inspiration issuing from those humble studios in which Gauguin and Van Gogh forgathered was to flood the world with a glory equalling Leonardo's. Cézanne believed that his canvases would find their way to the Louvre; he never suspected that reproductions of them would be welcomed in all the towns of America. Van Gogh had an inkling that he was a great painter, but not that fifty years after his death, he would be more famous than Raphael in Japan.

Doubtless Villon saw himself as both a vagabond and a great poet, but not as a genius reduced to felony by the supineness of the monarchy. And can one imagine Fouquet, his contemporary, setting himself up against Louis XI? Michelangelo quarrelled with the Pope, not with the papacy. Pheidias was no more an adversary of Pericles, or a Sumerian sculptor of King Gudea, than was Titian of his Republic, of Charles V, or Francis I. The break between the nineteenth century and a tradition that had lasted four thousand years was no less drastic and abrupt than that between the machine age and all previous ages. Was this only because the middle class was ceasing to understand art? But had the aristocracy understood it so well as all that? Were Géricault, Delacroix, Corot and Manet appreciated in Court circles, any more than by the working class? And did the latter understand Courbet's art? A great change had taken place; the artist no longer addressed himself to everyman, or to any given stratum of society, but solely to an elect few whose values were the same as his.

We have already seen how the artists joined forces and formed a society of their own, whose values were other than those of Society so-called; how mingled pride and resentment at feeling themselves "outcasts," led them to be a clan apart and dedicate their lives to an ideal — that of rivalling the Masters without imitating them. Aware of an immortality of which the beauty born on the shores of the Mediterranean had been but a fleeting expression, they applied themselves whole-heartedly to perpetuating that elemental and eternal language whose origins they were beginning to discern in the depths of the past.

Rarely have so many artists sacrificed so lavishly to an unknown god. Unknown, because those who served him, though intensely conscious of his presence, recognized it only in their own language, painting. Even the artists most disdainful of the *bourgeois* (i.e. the unbeliever), when in the act of painting their most ambitious pictures, could not adjust themselves without a qualm to the vocabulary truly capable of voicing their ambition, and, while devoted heart and soul to the noble task assigned them — that of creating a world of their own — they confined themselves to the jargon of craftsmen when they talked about it. Still, though none of them used the word "truth," all, in stigmatizing the works of their opponents, spoke of lies. When the expression "art for art's sake" came into vogue — evoking a smile from Baudelaire — what did it sponsor? Simply, the picturesque. But none is disposed to smile, now we are beginning to surmise that what is involved is neither art for beauty's sake, nor art for picturesqueness' sake, nor art for art's sake, but a power, more compelling than what was called beauty, which is wresting from time's sepulchres the buried works of art; and that this new faith, like the others, is claiming its eternity. Now that Romanesque, Egyptian, pre-Columbian arts are challenging traditional painting, and a new style is arising, the plastic arts, watching their history unfold before them, are learning that they transcend history. And the creation of painting that aspires to be painting and nothing else whatever, is likewise promoting a revival and a sense of brotherhood; for this painting is the language, still but partially deciphered, which the successive forms of the ephemeral have, unconsciously, employed. Though a thousand dead gods may have deceived the sculptors, sculpture did not deceive them, for it outlives the gods. That whole century, obsessed as it was with cathedrals, was destined to bequeath but one: the museum in which its paintings were to be assembled.

And in which they alone were assembled. When our Pantheon was due to be decorated, the government commissioned some talented artists, some mediocrities; as for Renoir and Cézanne, would they have been willing to take part? Painting, we have been told, has parted company with architecture; yet Cézanne's art is architectural, and Renoir's, when he chooses, can be more so than the Venetians', and at least as much so as Maillol's. It was not that Renoir was incapable of covering that splendid expanse of wall; it was "The Crowning of Charlemagne" that he could not, *would* not, paint. (The mere thought of it makes us smile!) But Delacroix would have painted it.

Whether or not Renoir endorsed the values which were to lord it in that egregious House of Fame, his painting had no truck with them; in his inner temple there was no place for a Pantheon like that, and even had he painted murals comparable to his sculpture, he could not have painted them without a feeling of discomfort. Even *The*

RENOIR. THE SPRING

RENOIR. THE SAÔNE AND THE RHONE

Saône and the Rhone, an admirable allegory that, however, plays fast and loose with history (a picture that he kept with him till his death), never got beyond the stage of a sketch. For this sketch was the real picture, and like all the moderns, Renoir was out to make *pictures,* more precisely paintings.

But what exactly is a modern picture? That term "cabinet-picture" covers a wide field: a Braque still life obviously differs *toto caelo* from one by a minor Dutch master; indeed a Cézanne still life was equally remote from it. These are not objects intended to be hung on a drawing-room wall, to ornament it — even if we do so hang them. It is on the cards that, thanks to a process of metamorphosis, Picasso may come to be regarded, in the year 2200, as a compeer of the Persian ceramists; but this will only mean that the critics of that day have lost the power of understanding the first thing about his art. The gestures we make in handling pictures we admire (not only master-pieces) are those befitting precious objects; but also, let us not forget, objects claiming veneration. Once a mere collection, the art museum is by way of becoming a sort of sanctuary. True, a Braque still life is not a holy object; yet, though no Byzantine miniature, it, too, belongs to another world, and a vaguely apprehended god, who goes by the name of Art, hallows it, even as the miniature was hallowed by the Pantocrator.

In this context the religious vocabulary is refractory; unfortunately we have no other. For this art is not a god, it is an absolute; but this absolute (which has its fanatics and martyrs) is no mere abstraction. The Independents, who spoke so charily of their art and so seldom laid down the law (not because they could not find the words: many of them wrote with remarkable precision), and whose congenial form of self-expression was the repartee, saw in the function attributed to art by their official adversaries (more than in their works, at which they merely mocked) not only a misconception but something positively repellent. The most zealous went so far as to frown upon even purely personal gestures which might seem to truckle to the enemy; thus Renoir's break with Degas was due to the insulting letter Degas sent him when he was awarded the Cross of the Legion of Honour (which he had never applied for). How could they have regarded an Impressionist who reverted to academic painting as other than a renegade? And with what less would they have visited him than with excommunication?

From the Romantic period onwards, art became more and more revered; the indignation felt at Van Eyck's being commissioned to design stucco decorations came from the feeling that this was nothing short of sacrilege. Else why be distressed by the thought that the great Italian Masters painted the figures on marriage-coffers, but not by the fact that they painted the figures on predellas? The artist's personal life had come to be regarded as a mere adjunct of his art. Such men as Leonardo and Velázquez, who painted only when called upon to do so, were very different from Cézanne, for whom painting was his life's *vocation*. Modern art, which has no longer an operative idea of Man, often suggests to us an operative idea of the artist.

What these modern artists, even when, like Manet, they were of middle-class extraction, loathed and condemned in the *bourgeoisie* was the values the *bourgeoisie* sought to substitute in art for those which formerly had enabled the painter to work at the service of an "absolute" — numinous, religious, revolutionary or legendary values; and, by the same token, they resented the fact that the *bourgeoisie* wished to forbid painting's becoming its own absolute. There was no longer any question of Vermeer's clandestine absolute; the artists made no secret of their intention to take charge of the situation, building anew the world that had vanished from Europe, a world that had known and venerated one supreme value. Less and less in the likeness of the world of appearances, the artist's vision harked back to the sacred figures of that autonomous world of art which had passed away. So now, like the African mask which does not represent a Negro but *is a spirit,* the picture no longer represented a certain scene, it *was a picture*; just that. The "otherness" which had played so great a part in sacred art, came back, but with a difference. This otherness, unlike that of the sacrosanct, did not derive from transcendence of the human; it stood for a world whence destiny was banished and in which man reigned supreme.

This would have been better understood, had not the religious element in art been confused, from the day of the Romantics and, above all, by them, with the powerful expression of some vague religious emotion. Nothing has misled our art-historians more than the Masses 'celebrated' by violonists in concert-halls beneath Beethoven's mask and facing plaster-casts of Michelangelo. The art which came to birth with Baudelaire and Manet was not put to the service of any such travesty of the absolute, but, rather, stepped into its — the absolute's — place.

It is no religion, but a faith. Not a sacrament, but a negation of the profane. Its rejection of appearance, its distortions, though they derive from a fervour very different from that inspiring the art of savages and even Romanesque art, are akin to these by reason of the intimate relation they establish between the painter and the object he creates. The modern picture aspires to union with a supreme value, on a higher plane than itself, not merely as did a picture by Raphael, but as a Romanesque figure of Christ claimed direct association with Jesus, the Son of God. Hence arose the curious mixture of acceptance and rejection of the world that we find in the art of the late nineteenth-century masters. Cézanne, Renoir and Van Gogh did not reject it as did Ivan Karamazov, but they rejected more than the mere social order; they repudiated passionately and conjointly the "soul" that men read into the visible world.

When modern artists deliberately change its appearance, this is in order to create another world which will serve their turn. Any talk of a modern art "of the masses" is but the expression of a desire to link up the taste for art with that for human brotherhood — a mere juggling with words. An art affects the masses only when it is at the service of *their* absolute and identified with it; when it produces Virgins, not statues. Thus, if he were in Russia, Picasso could portray Stalin only in a style repudiating that of all his pictures, *Guernica* included. For a modern artist, any genuine attempt to appeal to the masses would involve his "conversion" — a change of absolute. To whom, then, does he want to appeal? To those who are, more or less, of his own kind; and, in fact, their number is increasing. I have already suggested that Raphael would have understood the interest Van Gogh's painting might have for Van Gogh, but questioned the interest it could have for the average man. To-day we claim that Van Gogh's painting enables, not everyone, but a growing number of people to participate in a world which has once again found a supreme value; just as Raphael's painting enabled men of an earlier age to see the values that their culture stood for, expressed in the most satisfying form. But, as modern art forges ahead, it seems to become more and more indifferent to what art signified, whether deliberately or not, during untold ages: a form of man's awareness of the world. The sculptors of the Acropolis and the cathedrals, the painter of the Villeneuve *Pietà*, Michelangelo, Titian and Rembrandt really "possessed" a world; is not our art, born of a cleavage of man's consciousness, tending to "possess" no more than its private kingdom — that of painting?

VILLENEUVE PIETA (DETAIL)

V But the great sculptors, and Titian and Rembrandt, still transmit to us their possession of the world.

Once the specific language of painting had won its freedom from the extraneous, our culture saw endless vistas opening before it and, with these, hopes of a resuscitation ample yet selective, vying with the "closed" civilizations of the past on their highest level — and ever on the alert for rediscoveries sponsored by taste or by transfiguration. From the art of the Haida Indians to Coptic art, from that of the Hopi Indians to Gallic coins, the taste of our age rescues from oblivion every accent, angular or monumental, that conflicts with the arabesque and with the fluent modulation once so much admired. In the plastic arts, no less than in music, literature and the ballet, stridency and syncopation have become the order of the day. While some of the arts thus recalled to life have been so thoroughly incorporated into our culture as to transform it, others present themselves to us in the guise of new schools and, like them, either flourish or pass away. Thus our resuscitations sometimes answer to a modern craving for shrill-toned, experimental works which evoke new dialogues as it were with new-comers in the field of taste ; or else to another craving catered for — as by our famous European works of art — by such new works as evoke, like love, a dialogue that strikes ever deeper and indeed seems to us inexhaustible.

It is obviously on these latter that our culture is seeking to base itself, for it retains only that which stands up to time's attrition. But the dialogues they evoke are widely different in kind. No real "pluralism" was countenanced in Europe before we accepted simultaneously her Nordic and her Mediterranean traditions, as

ART OF HAIDA INDIANS

was done, not during the Renaissance, but when the primacy of Rome was seriously threatened by the coalition of the North, Venice and Spain — in the nineteenth century. Then, at last, despite the seemingly common "heritage" of Christendom, the sublimation of the forms of the earth challenged intimations of the supramundane, with Raphael and Praxiteles confronting Van Eyck and Grünewald ; then Autun and Egypt. And Rembrandt's shade, aware that Taine penned his *Philosophy of Art* so as to be able simultaneously to admire his, Rembrandt's, art and Raphael's, must smile at his encounter with Wei studies in the Metropolitan Museum, and in our memories.

Thus ours is the first culture to annex a host of vanished types of art whose function is radically different from that of its own art. Like the Gothics (though for other reasons) the Classical artists saw in art a complex of forms akin to each other and put to the service of accepted values ; then Romanticism put to the service of a Promethean concept of man, not one system only but a plurality of forms (though still akin); and, finally, our age seemed at first to seek to base the unity of all the arts it recognized as such on a kinship of forms *alone* ; thus it took to its bosom the pier-statue on the strength of its affinity with Cézanne. But, in our culture of to-day, the *Kings* of Chartres in no wise play the part of "abstract" statues ; they are incorporated in it precisely in so far as they do *not* play that part.

Though modern art, in virtue of the links between its style and styles remote in time, and of their common rejection of any cut-and-dry aesthetic (also in virtue of some vague notion of an identity of outlook), has blazed a trail by way of which a Wei statue naturally takes its place beside a Romanesque statue, the Wei figure has not thereby become a Romanesque queen or a modern statue — or even *only* a statue. Even now we can hardly bring ourselves to regard African masks as only cubist sculptures, with a difference. Our pluralism is not merely one of styles ; it covers also the functions of art, and while inextricably tangled up with art-history — indeed born alongside it — cannot come to terms with history without a struggle. Whenever Destiny or Becoming takes the place of Being, history takes the place of theology, and art comes to mean the sequence of works of art, a process of continual metamorphosis ; and these successive metamorphoses (not "art-history" in the sense in which this term is generally used) sponsor its march through Time.

Obviously Klee, and even Cézanne, do not strike us as being successors of the Masters of the past in the way that Raphael seemed a supreme fulfilment of the Quattrocentists ; nor is Velázquez seen as a precursor of Renoir. On the contrary, it is in so far as works of art, no matter how closely tied up with some specific period of the past, seem to claim an indisputable share in our culture of to-day, that the latter is acquiring its present form. A picture's past is neither wholly bound up with time, nor wholly a creation of the here and now. Indeed those living phantoms of the past that haunt us seem, no less than our contemporary art, expressions of our civilization.

Whether or not Suger and a peasant of his day liked the same statue, one thing is sure: both recognized one art only, Christian art. It cannot be too often repeated that the Renaissance did not see in the forms of classical antiquity those of a different world, valid in itself, and that all the popes, save Sixtus IV, collected "antiques" without any qualms of conscience. Nor were the poets appreciably paganized by their Nymphs; any more than was, later, Racine by Iphigenia. The Renaissance Masters vied with Antiquity and sought to annex it to their art, and in the Baroque scenes of martyrdom we have the *Laocoön's* aftermath. It was not the case that during the Renaissance a living art set itself up against an earlier art whose rôle had been the satisfaction of another part of the soul, now disdaining, now fraternizing with it. When ancients and moderns entered the lists, they still confronted masterwork with masterwork, indeed their kinship formed the common ground on which they clashed; in the company of Roman bas-reliefs, Poussin felt quite at home.

In our forefathers' time, the historical factor bulked little in the preference given to an Old Master, a Michelangelo or a Girardon. When Largillière saw *The Skate* and *The Buffet,* he said to Chardin: "Those Dutch were really great masters... Well, now let us have a look at your pictures." "But," replied Chardin, "they're *my* pictures." "To be sure!" And, quite unabashed, Largillière continued his inspection, approved of Chardin's standing for the Academy and voted in his favour. But how about us? We do not object to a picture's changing its maker (several Latours were ascribed to Le Nain, several Vermeers to other Hollanders), but we will not tolerate its changing its period; we do not mind a Rembrandt's looking modern, but resent a modern picture's looking like a Rembrandt. We assert that we would not admire *The Three Crosses* less were it anonymous. Anonymous, perhaps. But what if the etching, done by a less obvious genius, were a forgery? There is a disturbing ambiguity in the way we link up art with history, and it is not the theoretician who brings this home to us; it is the forger.

In classical aesthetics it was implied that the pastiche, carried to the point of perfection, might rank as a form of genius (though this raised awkward problems, since it involved deliberate adjustment to the original). Anyhow it was thought that a seventeenth-century sculptor might be able to turn out an even better *Apollo* than the Belvedere; thus the work of a forger of consummate ability would have gone on being approved of, even after the imposture was found out. Recognizing that the copy of the Portrait of Monsieur Bertin made by his pupil, Amaury Duval, was faithful to the original, Ingres actually consented to sign it. But we do not endorse his signature.

We admire a Greek archaic work, a Khmer head or a pier-statue only if we hold them to be genuine. A ring on the foot of one of the Parthenay *Kings* showed that the figure was a forgery; would it have become genuine for us again, had that foot been amputated?

While forgeries of the past aspired, through the pastiche, to attain genius, the impostor of to-day aspires to attain style through the riddle he sets the connoisseur.

No other modern forger can hold a candle to Van Meegeren. What exactly is the *Supper at Emmaus*? The disciple on the right is the portrait of a portrait, that of *The Geographer* and *The Astronomer* (the painter himself?), treated in Vermeer's technique, but also of some of Caravaggio's school (the "Pensionnante de Saraceni," for example); the man on the left forms a patch in the composition which may owe

VERMEER. THE GEOGRAPHER (FRAGMENT)

something to the *Soldier* in the Frick Collection. To copy the still life portion was almost as easy as copying the dottings on the bread, or Vermeer's monogram. There was no model for the figure of Christ in the work of Vermeer, who only portrayed Him once, at the close of his adolescence, in the Edinburgh *Martha and Mary*; so here Van Meegeren had a free field, enabling him to justify the strain of infidelity in his fidelity. The woman is taken over, rather awkwardly, from *The Procuress*; the colour of the other figures is obtained by a procedure used by counterfeiters in the domain of sculpture. They try to strike the right note by amplifying

some authentic detail of their victim's work. Here, noticing as all do, the very frequent association of blue and yellow in Vermeer's work, and having hit on the appropriate blue, Van Meegeren employs it as the basis of his picture, remakes a costume with that of the *Young Girl*, another with her turban, and adjusts the secondary tones — that of the woman excepted — to this colour harmony, the same as that of the *Young Lady in Blue* in the Rijksmuseum. In fact the entire colour-scheme brings to the rescue of the drawing (the most vulnerable and "tricky" element in Van Meegeren's enterprise) a "Vermeer" attuned to that colour harmony which is the first thing we think of when Vermeer is mentioned : a symbolical Vermeer, in short.

But a modernized Vermeer, and that is why the picture appealed to a wider public than Vermeer had ever reached, triumphed over Rembrandt in the Four Centuries of

Painting Exhibition, and was reproduced on calendars. The colour given the woman must have led even the casual observer to assume either that this figure was added (or subsequently repainted) or else to attribute to Vermeer the prescience of an art as yet unborn. A tempting theory (do not works of the past tend to appeal to us all the more strongly in so far as they seem anticipations of the future? Ossian's art would have been indeed prophetic; Macpherson's obviously was not); but a dangerous one. The composition is that of Caravaggio's *Supper at Emmaus* but "shot," as a cameraman might say, "in close-up"; that is to say it has become what it would be were the picture limited by a smaller frame. The result is that the frame cuts short all the figures adjoining it, depriving them of the air which would else have played around them — which in itself should have sufficed to rouse suspicions, since this method of "centering" does not belong to xviith-century art; and thus again it would have been prophetic — had it not been a fraud.

CARAVAGGIO (?). THE SUPPER AT EMMAUS

During his trial, Van Meegeren put forth a bold but futile plea; he claimed to rank beside Vermeer, in his own right. And, confronted by his *The Child Jesus and the Doctors*, not yet camouflaged with a semblance of antiquity, the experts were startled at discovering the face of a film "star" doing duty for that of Christ.

But the traditional forger does not really seek to imitate genius; he tries to copy its manner, or, when dealing with a period of anonymity, its style. And it is this latter which affects us so compellingly that all that bears its stamp passes as art. The Parthenay *Kings* were forgeries, but they did not lack style; and for a work to acquire style, it is enough for it to have struck deep roots in Time. What the antiquarians call styles are the "scripts" of the great men of the past. One of our counterfeiters who achieved a certain notoriety *sub rosa*, had the idea of weaving, then faking up, would-be mediaeval

VAN MEEGEREN. THE CHILD JESUS AND THE DOCTORS (DETAIL)

tapestries whose designs were a patchwork of authentic fragments; he filled the museums with them, then, on the point of being unmasked, committed suicide. Who would have questioned the Gothic style of these remarkable concoctions? In every line they featured the Gothic style — but the Gothic style alone. In some bogus Goya drawings there is not one stroke that is not copied from Goya. But, though these strokes have each and all made good in history, even the most meticulous, most happily inspired collation of them cannot evoke the world of *The Shootings of May 3*.

It may be suggested that the *Supper at Emmaus* could well claim a place beside some panel of a minor Dutch artist, as much influenced by his master as Van Meegeren was "influenced" by Vermeer. That is not so; Van Meegeren's picture is *dead*. And it is significant that an aesthetic as unsure of itself as ours should impose a death sentence on a painter not for his refusal to belong to his period (we tolerate this pretension on Ingres' part all the more readily because it is so ineffectual), but for his lying about his period.

The truth is that with the recognition of the autonomy of the specific language of the plastic arts came not only the discovery of their intonations but also that of their authentic voices. This would have been perceived sooner had not academicism professed to base its claims on the past, whereas the Independents, who resuscitated the past, staked theirs on the future. But the claim laid by the academics to even the most tradition-ridden past was growing less and less defensible; that, none the less, they held their ground so well was not due only to their readiness to truckle to the taste of the public, but also, and above all, to their ascribing to painting the same function that the public ascribed to it, a function which the masters of the past would never have endorsed. Hence their choice of subjects, ranging from would-be poetry to anecdotes, taking in battlepieces on the way. The struggle was so bitter, the genius of the Independents and the imposture of their opponents so plain to see (in the whole history of painting never had so contemptible a school been held in such esteem), that the mere notion of the "content" of the picture was engulfed in the derision heaped on those who set up to be its champions.

But that aspect of the Christian soul expressed by the Chartres *Kings,* of the Buddhist soul by a Wei or Khmer head, of the realm of magic by an African mask, had quite clearly nothing in common with the pictorialization of anecdotes or events of history. The "content" of Tintoretto is to be found less in his battle-scenes than in his nudes; indeed it is this which differentiates his nudes from those of Matisse (or Rembrandt). And it so happens that our retrospect embraces (and modern art has not brought forward) works of art that the spokesmen of officialdom had no claim to invoke on their behalf, nor did the Independents always invoke on theirs, yet lacking which our culture would not be what it is. A fervent and art-loving Christian of to-day finds in the masterpieces of the Middle Ages a supreme expression of his faith; now a faith such as Van Gogh's was, even in the xvth century, rare. Many works of the past respond to an emotion to which our contemporary art does not respond, and they respond to it in a language kindred to its own. All the works of art to which our culture clings (starting with those which our art has rescued from oblivion) have their word to say in the debate, and say it as vehemently as did the works of the classical past in the xvith century. For modern art set out to be a revolution, whose aim, however, was a restoration — the re-enthronement of *true* painting. If, in some of its aspects, it is harsh and bigoted, this is not because our art of to-day opposes the "resurrection" of the past, but on the contrary, because it has emerged simultaneously with it, swept into the light on the same wave. And, if in it man has lost his visage, the culture sponsoring this disfigured man has retrieved the noblest visages that the world has ever seen — and forgotten.

If we picture a great artist acquainted, in addition to contemporary works, with only the specifically plastic qualities of the works of the past, we would write down that man as the higher type of the modern barbarian : one whose barbarianism is not, as in an earlier time, definable by his rejection of the status of the citizen, but, rather, by his rejection of the estate of man. Had our culture to be restricted to our sensitivity (keen though it is) to forms and colours, and the expression of these in our modern forms of art — surely such a culture would be literally inconceivable. But it is far from being thus restricted. For an art culture without precedent is taking form : one in which the values expressed by living works of the past and contemporary art are no longer, as they were so often, similar, but rather — shall we say ? — complementary.

When Western civilization ceased being regulated first by an all-powerful hierarchy of religious values, then by an hierarchy of cultural values, the highest manifestations of the human spirit outside the Western world were no longer disparaged. Thus Indian temples ceased being dubbed "pagodas," the Indians being called "heathens," while, similarly, "Gothic" ceased to be an epithet applied to bunglers, and "quaint" to some Dutch artists. The dialogue that now began between the *Summa Theologica* and the Vedanta evokes an echo in our minds of those famous debates between Buddhists and Greek sages at King Menander's court. Synchronizing with the weakening of Christendom and even of Christianity, the rise to power of history is due neither to modern science nor to research-work into the lives of Christ and Buddha, but to the fact that history neatly assigns each religion to the appropriate pigeon-hole of a restricted period, and so makes it relative. Thus it loses its value as an absolute — a value which syncretic systems, such as theosophy, are obviously unable to replace. Indeed that absolute had ruled out any possibility of effective intercourse ; Islam, in the age of Bajazet, had not been an amiable hypothesis but an instant threat : and, as such, abominated.

Though we have not adopted the gods of other races, they have ceased to be regarded as heathen devils and have become forms ; yet, since these are not abstract forms, they have not wholly lost their significance along with their divinity — even when that significance is suggested, rather than transmitted to us as it is by the holy figures of the Egyptian theogony. Whenever, thanks to some telling accent, some wealth of suggestion or effect of starkness, the language of a work of art appeals to us, we listen to it as to the voice of an artist who, nameless though he be, is hallowed in our eyes by the spiritual values he expresses. We are fully aware that behind a Khmer head lie centuries of Buddhism, yet, when looking at it, we yield to an impression that its spirituality and splendour must have been a *trouvaille* of its sculptor. It suggests to us a "relativized absolute." We look at great works of religious art less as what they are than as so many Zarathustras invented by so many Nietzsches. Much as the Christianity of the Renaissance christianized the forms of classical antiquity (which transformed its art), we restore to Man all the forms of bygone grandeur that once were his.

Why is it that the German theory of "cultures," meaning independent civilizations that flourish and pass away, like living organisms, has won such general acceptance, especially when drained of the precision its exponents sought to give it? Because, by subordinating religion to an organic living entity which gave birth to it, this theory can, in its dialectics with religious civilizations, leave the religion out, without, moreover, limiting itself to forms. That myth of self-contained cultures is but a vehement projection of the modern spirit across the vista of the past. The pre-Columbian religions are known only to specialists, and those who respond to Indian art are more numerous than adepts of the Vedanta. For the last thirty years the Orient and its legend have been declining on the status of a standardized "Antiquity." But the strange metamorphosis which enables us to annex the arts of the past also enables those which we recall to life to reach our culture bearing messages that our own art rejects.

Not all religions (as I have already said) make their appeal to the same facet of the soul. The reason Europe misunderstood so long those of the past, was that she was trying to bring them into line with her own faith. How understand what Buddhism is, if we imagine that "Buddhists *worship* Buddha?" Or what their religion meant to the Greeks, if we see in the gods of Olympus either a multiplied Trinity or a horde of fetishes? Religions resemble each other in respect of all that puts the gods at the service of men (there is always a godling for the recovery of lost umbrellas), not in respect of that which puts men to the service of the gods.

The Wei Bodhisattvas, the great Khmer sculptured figures and Sung paintings do not convey the same communion with the transcendent as does a Romanesque tympanum, a Dance of Siva, or the horsemen of the Parthenon. Yet all these works express a communion of one kind or another, differing thus from works that express none. While it is impossible to draw a clear dividing line between these two categories (as, indeed, between most categories of art), the contrast between different complexes of forms — works that press downwards and works that soar, classical and romantic art, and so forth — plays a less important part in our culture than does the conflict between works of art that seem to restrict themselves to Man (as do, conspicuously, modern works of art) and — all the others. There is by no means the same difference between Rembrandt and Vermeer as between Rembrandt and the Villeneuve *Pietà*, or the Panathenaic frieze.

Here there is no question of religion, unless we mean by "religion" all that buoys man up on the dark flood of the unknown. Is that cosmic Bacchanalia, Rubens' *Kermesse*, a religious work? However thorough-going its triumph over the mystery-laden East, it is plain to see that any masterpiece of Greek art owes its triumph not to Greek rationalism but, rather, to "the innumerable laughter of the sea."

Like a muted orchestra, the surge and thunder, already so remote, of ancient tragedy accompanies the cry of Antigone echoing through the ages : "I was not born to share in hatred, but to share in love." Greek art is not an art of solitude but one of a communion with the cosmos, from which Rome was to sever it. No deep communion is limited to sentiment; Christianity and Buddhism gave rise to sentimental arts, but, once Christ discarded, we have not been given another Chartres or another Rembrandt; we were given Greuze. The great arts of communion, like the religions associated with them, are mediations between man and the infinite, enabling him to feel he is more than a chance by-product of the universe.

Though the Middle Ages did not regard themselves as a phase of history, they struck root in the depths of a past very different from the historic past, and one from which they could not even conceive of themselves as being detached ; and this holds good to-day for Islam and India — where India and Islam still exist, as such. Their here-and-now (like the "time" of "In that time...") is a moment of the eternal. The Renaissance replaced this eternity with much less than is supposed of classical antiquity, even in those countries where this replacement touched its maximum. It was only when at last the link was broken which, by way of a communion (not a birthright), across centuries whose "history" was mere synopsis or chronology, had united men to Mother Earth as to the Hero, to Venus as to Christ — it was only when this link was broken that the supreme value of art as something existing in and for itself was first glimpsed, then boldly proclaimed.

The dialogue in progress between our culture and all those transient absolutes which the resuscitated arts transmit to us, is restoring the links with a past to which it is giving shape : the link between the Greek gods and the cosmos, and that between Christ and the meaning of this world and all the souls of the living and the dead. Every Sumerian work evokes a kingdom of Sumer, grasped in part by us, eluding us in part. The great museums, while catering to our craving for the exotic, give us the run of a vast realm of human aspiration and achievement; but the long trail that human sensibility has blazed there is other than that of history. It is not dead communities that art recalls to life ; it is often some idealized, or compensating, picture of themselves they wishfully built up, and always a picture of a nature other than in reality theirs was.

There is here no more any question of embellished cultures than of embellished figures. The Goyas of the Deaf Man's House are not embellished nightmares ; they are pictures. The blood-smeared sacrificial fetish is not a savage; the modelled and painted death's-head, not a skull ; and, wretched as was the art of Rome in the tenth century, it does not show us that hapless John XVI, his eyes gouged out, his nose cut off, whom the other pope, the victor, forced to listen to the gibes of the populace and to sing, through his mutilated lips, until nightfall, "It is just that I be treated thus!"

The mosaics of Byzantium do not portray tortures, nor the best Aztec carvings, massacres. The ghastliness of the most violently Spanish *Crucifixions* differs fundamentally from a scene of wanton cruelty. Always, however brutal an age may actually have been, its style transmits its music only; the art museum is the song of history, not its news-reel.

We speak of the past as though we saw it planted in our culture, like an ancient monument in a modern city; yet we know full well that this is not the case. For a small minority, keenly interested in history, it is fraught with meaning, and its elucidation means a gradually won victory over chaos. For the vast majority it comes to life only if it be transformed into some gigantic legend, 'fictionalized': but what foundation is there for such presentations? What do Greece, Rome, the Middle Ages really mean to us save statues, edifices and poetry (meaning more than "verses")?

"That the name of Alexander rings through the centuries with a clang of bronze is due far less to his campaigns than to the undying dream he conjures up, a dream whose each expression gives him a new lease of fame. So long as the artists pay no heed to him, a conqueror is a mere victorious general; Caesar's relatively small conquests are nearer to our minds than all Genghiz Khan's far-flung triumphs. It is not the historian who confers fame; it is the poet with his power over the dreams of men."

For it is art whose forms suggest those of a history which, though not the true one, yet is that which shapes men's ends. Living, the great Romans would not have swayed the Convention as Plutarch did; nor would the Greeks of old, did they return to life, influence Europe as do their statues and Acropolis. In the same sense as that in which Amphitrite was the goddess of the sea, who made the waves benign to men, the art of Greece is for us the true god of Greece. This god it is, and not the lords of Olympus, who shows us Greece in her noblest aspect, triumphant over time and near us even to-day, for it is through her art alone that Greece invites our love. Many arts have had their tutelary gods, but Apollo, the immortal, still looks superbly down on the dead gods of Tyre, who disdained poems and statues. All arts are the divine intercessors of human civilizations: the deities of a strange polytheism.

And some of them, like certain other gods, are all the more potent for the mystery enveloping them.

That curious fascination exercised by the works of half-caste civilizations does not always come from their plastic qualities. The Cham Sivas of Turania, with their

CHAM ART (IXth CENT.). SIVA

hybrid art, conjure up a soul in which Malay refinement thrusts up through a savage mental undergrowth, as, in the jungle clearings, its temples rise through a glittering haze of giant spiders' webs. The "poetry" of this art is that of the great frontiers, where Java merges into Polynesia, China into the Steppes, Egypt into Greece, Byzantium into Persia, or Islam into Spain, Spain into Mexico. Almost it has the quality of those works of art which give hints of the spirit of communities dimly known, if known at all : prehistoric paintings, then plaques, or Manichean miniatures — and the proto-Etruscan *Warrior of Capistrano*. Gazing at that enigmatic figure, as when we gaze at cave paintings and so many illustrations of texts for ever lost, how can we fail to hear a voice, calling across the ages, like the call that sounded once across enchanted seas, attuned in some elusive manner to that aura with which genius is ever widening our awareness, and to that stately peal of silver bells which Michelangelo launches above the tombs of Florence ? History is at once a restless probing of the past and a will to render it intelligible ; a museum is the muster of a world as dissimilar from the real world as the work of art is from the real. From the inscrutable recession of the ages, it brings back the flotsam of a visionary past which, out of so many gods and devils, has bequeathed only that which was scaled down to the human.

When historians took to vaticination (as they so often do), the past became protean. Thus we are given an interpretation of the Middle Ages according to Michelet, and one of Greece according to Taine ; also by Michelet we are shown a French Revolution, which is a more successful picture than his Middle Ages because it is an admirable and impassioned rendering of a collective emotion around which it weaves a myth. But while we have likewise a mythical Greece invented (less vigorously) by Renan to illustrate a Golden Age, there was another Greece — the Greece of Pheidias. And likewise, apart from the myth Romanticism has foisted on the Middle Ages, we have — the cathedrals. And in the retrospect of art, Sumer, Babylon, Nineveh, Teotihuacàn have come to mean to us the hymns rising out of the darkness of their past ; the sordid history of Byzantium is submerged by the majesty of the Pantocrator ; that of China by the Tao and Buddha's meditation ; the squalor of the Steppes, by the gold plaques ; the lazar-houses of the Middle Ages by the *Pietàs*. Living humanity transmits inexorably its monsters with its blood, yet the genius of dead Assyrian artists, when it hands down to us the horrors of that grim régime, the kings who blinded their victims figuring on the bas-reliefs, fills our memories, to the exclusion of the rest, with the majesty of the *Dying Lioness*. I have seen the fetishes of the Nuremberg Museum justify their age-old leer as they gazed down at wisps of smoke curling up from the ruins, through which a girl on a bicycle, carrying a sheaf of lilac, steered an erratic course amid singing Negro truck-drivers ; but were there an art of the prison-camp incinerators, only that day extinguished, it would show us not the murderers, but their victims.

ASSYRIAN ART (VIIth CENT. B.C.). THE DYING LIONESS

On this plane the *Koré of Euthydikos* becomes the sister of the Perpignan *Christ in Prayer*. That transfigured world which styles reveal to us (yet more transfigured in the case of masterpieces) is no longer restricted to what it was when it arose. The figures of the Old Kingdom, the Delphi *Charioteer*, the *Lady of Elche*, a Chinese or Khmer Bodhisattva, the Chartres *David*, *Uta*, the *Christ* of Rheims, and *The Thinker*, a pre-Columbian figure and even *The Beggar Woman*, like Van Eyck's *Adam* and Masaccio's, the Villeneuve *Pietà* and the Isenheim Altar, Giotto's *Nativity* and Michelangelo's *Creation of Adam*, Titian's Venice *Pietà* and *The Three Crosses* or *The Burial of Count Orgaz*, the best paintings of the Sung artists and the best of Ajanta — all these have one feature in common : their submission to the dialogue, proud or pensive, maintained by each of them with that portion of his soul the artist deems the loftiest. Dialogues hardly more clearly linked up with the religions that gave them rise than is the *Vita Nuova* with Beatrice, the *Tristesse d'Olympio* with Juliette Drouet. In them religions are but the highest realms of the human ; for those who believe that Christian art was called into being by Christ, do not believe that Buddhist art was called into being by Buddha, Sivaic forms by Siva. They are at one with the triumphal march of the Panathenaic frieze, the cosmic frenzies of Rubens' *Kermesse*, the brooding horror of *The Shootings of May 3* — and perhaps with the purity of heart, nameless as yet, that Cézanne and Van Gogh brought into painting. And across this stately progress, in which the gods march side by side with man in a fraternity at last accepted, there is now beginning to emerge that which the gods sometimes incarnated, sometimes fought down, sometimes submitted to, which we call Destiny.

Only too well we know that this word derives its potency from its expression of our dependence, the mortal element of all that is doomed to die. There is a "fault" (as a geologist would call it) in our spiritual stratum, from which no god can always guard us ; the saints call it a "dryness of the soul," and, for Christendom, that cry "Why hast Thou forsaken me ?" is the most human of all cries. Time flows — perhaps towards eternity ; inevitably towards death. But Destiny is not death ; it consists of all that forces on us the knowledge of our nothingness, and, to begin with, of our loneliness. This is why, seeking escape, man has so often made love his refuge ; and it is why religions defend man against Destiny (even when they do not defend him against death) by uniting him with God or with the cosmos. That part of man which yearns for transcendence and for immortality is familiar to us. We know, too, that a man's awareness of himself functions through channels other than those of his awareness of the outside world ; every man's self is a tissue of fantastic dreams. I have written elsewhere of the man who fails to recognize his own voice on the gramophone, because he is hearing it for the first time through his ears and not through his throat ; and because our throat alone transmits to us our inner voice I named the book *La Condition Humaine (Man's*

Fate). In art the other voices do but ensure the transmission of this inner voice. The artist's message owes its force to the fact that it arises from the very heart of silence, from a devastating loneliness that conjures up the universe so as to impose on it a human accent; what survives for us in the great arts of the past is the indefeasible inner voice of civilizations that have passed away. But this surviving, no more immortal, voice soaring towards the gods, needs for its accompaniment the tireless orchestra of death. Our awareness of destiny, as profound as that of the Orientals but covering a far vaster field of reference, stands in the same relation to the various "fates" of the past as does a modern museum to the "Collections of Antiquities" of our forefathers; those wraith-like marble forms have given place to this Revelation of our century, the "Museum without Walls," and there is tentatively taking form, for the first time on earth, the concept of a worldwide humanism.

Whether that humanism is to make good or come to nothing, one element of it, an all-embracing art culture, is developing under our eyes. A culture, not a history or encyclopaedia of art. The link between art and the values of its period (like that between it and the artists' lives) is becoming very different, for us, from that which the xixth century thought to have established. Even as Goya defied syphilis by recapturing nightmare visions of unremembered time, and Watteau fought consumption with melodious dreams of beauty, so some civilizations seem to defend themselves against destiny by allying themselves with the cosmic rhythms, and others by repudiating them. Nevertheless, in our eyes, the art of both has this in common, that it expresses a *defence* against fatality; though the company of statues in the cathedrals is a Christendom without sin, it expresses, for non-Christians, not so much Christ as the defence, by Christ, of Christians against destiny. Hitherto, all civilizations that built up a past to sponsor them, peopled it with congenial exemplars; whereas our art culture makes no attempt to search the past for precedents supporting its solutions, but it transforms the entire past into a series of tentative and transient answers to a problem that remains intact.

The truth is that our civilization, mighty as it is, differs from all preceding it — save the Greek — in not being affirmative. Like its sciences, it is interrogative; and our art, too, is becoming an interrogation of the world.

Never, indeed, since the Renaissance, has interrogation abrogated its supremacy, save in appearance. Thus the ornate shadow of Versailles, lengthening out across the whole seventeenth century, tends to hide from us its harassed soul; and under the rich profusion of the Jesuit churches the rifts in Christendom were ever widening. Leonardo had been interrogation incarnate, yet this enabled him to come to terms with the universe on, as it were, Far-Eastern lines — a pact of which his drawings of waves may seem the symbol. Later, when that spirit of interrogation probed deeper, until man was no longer an ally of the world of things but its enemy — when, with the factory replacing the cathedral, the artist felt himself excluded from the new world man had won — the history of art became the story of the annexation of the world by the individual. We are told that art has touched its limit; its expression can go no farther. That has often been said; but even if it can go no farther, it yet may go elsewhere. The great religious art of Christendom did not die because all possible forms had been used up; it died because Faith was waning. Now the same conquest of the world of things that gave rise to our modern individualism (so different from that of the Renaissance), is by way of "relativizing" the individual. It is, in fact, indisputable that man's faculty of transformation began by remaking the pattern of the natural world, and has ended by calling man himself in question. Still too strong to be a slave, and not strong enough to remain a king, the individual, while by no means willing to abandon his conquests, is ceasing to find in them his *raison d'être*; the "devalued" individual of the five-year plans and the Tennessee Valley is losing nothing of his strength, but individualist art is losing its power to annex the world.

Thus it is that the spirit of questioning is stealing a march on annexation; Picasso following Cézanne. And thus it is that the negative values which play so great a part in our civilization as well as in our art, are coming to the fore. Thus it is that the fetishes are entering our culture; for the fetish-maker they were not necessarily interrogative, but, for us, they are. In all our art, even the least aggressive — that of Renoir, or of Braque — there is implied a challenge, ever more strongly voiced, of a world that it disclaims. Its struggle against "appearance," against any presentation ordered by values other than those of art, should be enough to make this plain; we refuse, as emphatically as Byzantium refused, to be ruled by appearance. Whereas Van Gogh saw in himself the harbinger of an art to be, in which the lost plenitude of the past would re-emerge, Picasso knows that it would re-emerge *against* him. But for the painter always his art comes first; inseparable from the will to art, his interrogation serves him as a means of implementing it, and the same holds good for the poets. Shakespeare's interrogation is the source of his noblest poetry; however charged with emotion is Dostoevsky's narrative, it changes its nature and becomes art in the scene where Muishkin and Rogojin are keeping vigil over Nastasia Philippovna's dead body; indeed Dostoevsky himself wrote, "The main thing is to make my *Brothers Karamazov* a work of art." And so it is that all that humanity remembers of that insatiable interrogation which was the soul of Greece, is a triumphal affirmation.

There lies behind all art (as behind every form of poetry) a calling-in-question, sometimes docile, sometimes rebellious, of the world; and our modern art's indictment is the least docile, the most aggressive, that the world has seen. It is the art of a period during which the sciences have derived their alarming power from this ruthless interrogation of the universe. But though a "power civilization" can exist, no culture can exist based solely on interrogation.

Culture consists of all that enables man to enrich, or to transform without impairing it, the ideal vision of himself he has inherited. That is why the most searching arraignment of the world humanity has known is promoting a worldwide resuscitation. This, too, is why, in seeking to escape from its perplexities and narrowness, and take its place in culture properly so called, our artistic culture comes up against what our fathers called "the masterpiece."

Neither studio cliques, nor modern styles, have succeeded in dethroning the *Monna Lisa*. For it is not so easy as all that to classify the picture as "academic"; to what other artist's work is it akin? To Bouguereau's, for instance? That traditional admiration which sets it on a pedestal as "the world's most beautiful picture," is based on a misunderstanding, which, incidentally, accounts for the frequent dismay of the tourists visiting the Louvre — but leaves the picture exactly where it was. When we compare it with such charming productions of Leonardo's disciples as Melzi's *Columbina* or Luini's *Salome,* and if we try to discover what exactly it is that distinguishes it from works formerly ascribed to Leonardo, we find that not only purely pictorial qualities differentiate it from its feebly inspired posterity. Yet Leonardo's best disciples lacked neither poetry nor a sense of mystery. Psychology, then? A theory has been mooted, and backed by solid arguments, that the sitter for this picture was not Monna Lisa at all, but Costanza d'Ávalos. Now the expression of the lady of high Florentine society, whose smile, a legend tells us, was "held" by Leonardo over a period of four years, by having musicians and buffoons perform at each sitting, is most unlikely to have been that of the heroic woman who defended Ischia against the armies of the King of France. Still, whichever woman we think to see in the picture, its quality remains the same; and we need but recall the work of lesser Milanese painters to feel the supreme intelligence, not of the undetermined model, but of assuredly the subtlest homage that genius ever paid to a once living face. And what irony that this intelligence, of which none ever speaks, should thus uphold in secret so great a glory!

While the last noises of the day are dying out in a threatened Paris which, too, perhaps, is drawing to its end, the words of Leonardo echo in my memory: "Then it befell me to make a truly divine painting. . ." True, there are others we prefer; but how many convey the same sense of victory? We are beginning to discern what it is that unequivocally distinguishes such works from creations which merely satisfy the cravings of the sensibility, even at its keenest, most receptive; in them the artist has broken free from destiny with such compelling power that they transmit the echo of his liberation to all who understand their message. Thus posterity, for the artist, means the gratitude of men for victories which seem to promise them their own.

As long as the work of art was regarded as a "product," as long as determinisms and conditionings held sway, art was seen as being subservient to history. But once we realize that the creative stimulus, far from being implicit in the historical *processus,* the chain of causes and effects, is a deliberate break with it, we find that art, if still involved in history, is linked with it in a manner that is the opposite of what was once assumed. The link that the forger so pertinently forces on our notice does not tie up the artist with world history, but with *the history of forms*. We do not object to the *Supper at Emmaus* because it was painted in our time and not in the seventeenth century at Delft; we object to it on the strength of all the successive forms which have ensued since Vermeer's death. Recently there has been discovered the art of Dvaravati, a little-known kingdom on the shores of the Gulf of Siam, in which, during the seventh century, Buddhist figures (of Gupta origin) attained a quality ranking them beside the best Khmer figures. Formerly they were ascribed to the Thai art of Lop Buri; later, to Khmer art. But their new, well-authenticated ascription puts an end to our misgivings and confirms the genius that went to their making. Yet we know almost nothing of the Dvaravati civilization (which indeed plays no part in this connexion). Thus, too, it came as a relief to learn that Grünewald, having been born much earlier than was supposed (his real name being Neithardt), had quite possibly been Dürer's master, certainly not his disciple. The truth is that while every great work of the past strikes us as expressing or implying its period, always there is implicit in it an element of conquest. Bad pictures, too, express their period. But the artist of genius does not passively receive from the visible world the forms enabling him to conquer and possess a self-sufficing, coherent kingdom all his own; he has to wrest them from the outside world, and this victory over his individual human destiny, spreading like ripples on the sea of time, merges into art's eternal victory over the destiny of mankind.

All history is the record of an evolution or fatality made intelligible; all history tends to interpret the past in terms of destiny — whether fraught with hope, as in the case of Bossuet, Hegel and Marx, or with death, as was the case with Spengler. Whereas an authentic history of art (not a chronology of influences) can no more be the record of a progress than (in its strict sense) that of an "eternal return"; art is the arch-enemy of destiny. True, even a rupture has its limits; El Greco did not break free from Titian by painting Renoirs. Nevertheless, while his subjection to Titian belongs to historical fatality, his works do not belong to it; indeed the whole history of art, where genius is concerned, should be a record of deliverance. For, while history seeks merely to transform destiny into awareness, art seeks to transmute it into freedom.

The life of art does not illustrate man's course through Time as a one-way progress, but as a putting forth or fanning-out of his powers in various directions. It consists of continuities (sometimes rigidly precise) operating within a permanent discontinuity. Little does art heed the death of civilizations: in periods when the Present holds the field, it is nourished by the Present; in others it grows from a dialogue that transforms the Past, as rites of the forest hallow the trees with sanctity. Its essential unity through the ages comes primarily from the methods by which it annexes the world — insensate though they sometimes seem. Though a Byzantine mosaic and a Rubens, a Rembrandt and a Cézanne, do not affect us as portrayals of scenes, each of these works sponsors a mastery distinct in kind and imbued in its distinctive manner with that which has been mastered by the artist. But all unite with the artists of the Magdalenian epoch in speaking the language of man's conquest, though the *terrain* conquered was not the same. For us the message of the Wei Buddhas is not an evangel of Buddhism, nor that of the Sivaic Dancer of Death one of Hinduism; indeed the message of all masterpieces consists, essentially, in the simple fact of their existence. And in an agnostic civilization who but must have recourse to that part of himself which transcends, and often uplifts, himself? The quality of Man, and not the mere amassing of knowledge, is the supreme aim of every culture, and our art culture knows that it cannot restrict itself to tempering, however exquisitely, our sensibility; it aspires to the heritage of what is noblest in the world, now that it is discovering a nobility of the world of which it is the sole heir.

Thus, in times when man feels stranded and alone, art means for its votaries a communion or a transfiguration inherited from those which the departing gods no longer hallow. When we introduce into our civilization so many hostile elements, how fail to see that our eclecticism, defying history, merges them into a past that is wholly "positivist," and whose whole conception is alien to the real past? Under the beaten gold of those Mycenean masks where we once looked to find only the dust of a dead beauty, there was throbbing a secret power, whose rumour, echoing down the ages, at last we hear again. And issuing from the shadows of the tombs, muffled voices of the Memphian Empire make answer to Klee's gossamer brushstrokes and the blue of Braque's grapes. Let us make no mistake as to this company of shadows that is rising from the sands; if we wrest from the ruins of the past whatever forms attest the human, it is not in order to submit ourselves to them, but to annex them.

Our resurrection began with modern art. The form under which we know it nears its end; brought into being, like the philosophy of the "Enlightenment," by a conflict, it cannot outlive its victory without undergoing a metamorphosis. But while it declines, our "resurrection" of the past is ever covering a wider field, as did the "resurrection" of Antiquity when the Renaissance had spent its force, and that of Gothic after the passing of Romanticism. Our problems are not those of Babylon, Alexandria or Byzantium; even if it is doomed to be exterminated to-morrow, our civilization will not have been that of Egypt on the brink of death; nor is the hand which is feverishly wresting from the earth the buried past the hand that shaped the last Tanagras; at Alexandria the museum was but an Academy of Art. This civilization of the conquest of the globe calls for a metamorphosis as drastic as those associated with the great religions, and it may be that we should see in man's discovery of fire the only precedent to the mechanization of to-day. For the first time the link uniting agricultural civilizations, as mother earth unites the forests and the graves, is broken. When the Greek spirit was at its freest, the Greeks felt as much at home at the court of the Achemenides as did the Byzantines at the Sassanian court; photographic reconstitutions of a Roman street with its shops and stalls, its veiled women and men in togas, conjure up less a London street than a street in Benares; when they discovered Islam, our romantic artists thought to have before them a living picture of the ancient world. Our age is the first to have lost its share of Asia. This first worldwide art culture, which is bound to transform modern art (by which until now it was given its lead), is not an invasion, but one of the crowning conquests of the West. Whether we like it or not, the West will light its path only by the torch it carries, even if it burns its hands, and what that torch is seeking to throw light on, is everything that can enhance the power of Man.

Rome welcomed in her Pantheon the gods of the defeated.

COMPLEMENTARY
STUDIES

NOTE

For the full understanding of the following complementary studies, they should be intercalated at their respective places (indicated by the sub-titles in italics). They are not studies of Christian origins and Celtic coins. Nor were the passages in The Creative Act *concerning El Greco and Tintoretto studies of these painters; they were analyses, by way of these artists, of the relations between the painter and the scenes of life; similarly, the pages here devoted to Georges de Latour are an analysis of the relation between the painter and the works of art he sets out to transform.*

FIRST STUDY

Addendum to the study of the development of Christian art

CATACOMB OF DOMATILLA. PRAYING WOMAN

THAT deeply moving quality of the paintings in the Catacombs comes not from their value, but from their speaking with the halting accents of Man making his timid answer to the thunders of Sinai. When some monk in everyday attire, carrying a little candle fixed to the end of a broom-stick, shows us the first inscriptions, how fail to hear again that voice arising from the depths ? It is the selfsame ageless voice we hear as we thread our way between the rocks in the Font-de-Gaume cave, and come on the

CATACOMB OF DOMATILLA (IInd CENT.). GOOD SHEPHERD (?)

timeworn shapes of the bison, wavering in the torchlight as if they were their shadows. If in the art of the Catacombs that elemental magic of the age of stone when man's death was a finale without hope, is lacking, present in it is a voice promising deliverance from death, the voice of a Revelation, and of a forgiveness. Yet how faltering seems the response of these humble figures to that august voice! Above ground, beyond the plains of the Campagna, stretch stately avenues of cypresses in dark recession, while the sun still pounds on his anvil the red gold that shimmered in the Roman air when Anthony's ship set sail towards his "Egypt"; but underground the unnumbered dead, the martyrs, and the Revelation that was to triumph over the Empire have left but a few pathetic figures — and a poor imitation of the *décor* of Nero's villa.

In second-century Rome it would seem that style had ceased to be a means of expression; the sarcophagi of pagans, Jews and Christians, the bas-reliefs depicting whether the emperors' victories or the sacrificial rites of Mithra, all pertain to the same art. Indeed the Christian soul ensconced itself in antique forms, as naturally as, later, were to do the churches in the palaces of the Caesars.

It was at first the clumsiness, the poverty of their art, that gave the Catacombs their specifically Christian accent. It would be pleasant to read a meaning into this poverty, to glimpse behind the graffiti of Good Shepherds that tragic, passionate figure whose touching copy they might be; actually, the figures on the sarcophagi, the Good Shepherd, the Praying Woman, derive from Flavian figures. It was not so as to break away from the imperial style that they developed into signs; they followed it in many cases. And in this underworld of tombs that Rome-inspired picture of *Autumn* toys with the dying Empire.

AUTUMN (CA. 240)

In any case, Shepherds, Praying Women, the Lord's Supper, sometimes belong to the same realm of art as do the bread broken at that Supper, the fishes, the pathetically uncouth crosses. Then, as their calligraphy developed, it began to reject the forms of Antiquity, but often only to replace them by those of its minor arts. The Christian painters were artisans and, then as now, the forms of decoration were not always those of art.

Yet though the inexpertness of this calligraphy reduces it to *décor*, it is more than decorative; its very poverty gives it a curious starkness, if not a style. Some of those Praying Women seem on the point of voicing the holy love encompassing them in death's long night, and some few figures seem trying to shelter in a meshwork of dark lines all these humble folk, bewildered as imprisoned children. And now the painters came up against a problem that other Christian artists were soon to tackle: how to portray the holiest figures of all. To begin with, the use of the sign (to the exclusion of portrayal) for their Good Shepherds, even the most realistic, seconded their humility. Later, when the Good Shepherd frankly became Christ and the woman with the child the Madonna, two methods of expression lay open to the artist.

At Byzantium the usage of a broken line came gradually to temper (especially in ivory paintings) the inherent heaviness of Constantinian art; though this was not so at first. The *Christ with Four Saints and the Apostles* of the Catacomb of Domatilla clearly owes more to engraving than to sculpture. It is well known that all this art came to acquire a Byzantine accent, and the stages of the progress are well marked. But the life-story of Roman art during this period is far from consisting solely of the factors transforming it into Byzantine art; sometimes it tells of a struggle with the East, whose pressure was already felt. Long before Byzantium weighed on the Roman world, a dogged effort was being made at Rome to achieve a local expression of

CATACOMB OF DOMATILLA. CHRIST WITH FOUR SAINTS AND THE APOSTLES (CA. 348)

CATACOMB OF PRISCILLA. THE VIRGIN (IIIrd CENT.)

Christianity; to begin with, by substituting a faltering, perhaps, yet fervid will to personal style for the conceptions which had made Roman style an idealization of the Roman myth. Lines that had served to express Mars or Venus were certainly the devil's; and though it was yet to be discovered which were God's, there was always the resource of exorcising those smoothly flowing, diabolic lines by the use of angular, abrupt brush-strokes unknown to the ancients. And this broken line was not yet the scythe-blade notch of the Byzantines. That unknown man who painted the *Woman with the Child* in the Catacomb of Priscilla was perhaps the first Christian artist.

However, Rome retained her old love of the portrait, and in the cemeteries the gilt-glass portraits kept up her tradition of photographic likeness. Yet now eternal life came to impart a new accent to the individual face, as the proximity of the corpse was to do in the Fayum. (We can hardly picture the *Poetess* of Pompeii painted on a winding-sheet.) Some of these Praying Women became portraits sublimated by the enlarging and fixity of the eyes. And once angular linework was combined with this otherworldly gaze, a truly Christian style came into being.

Meanwhile, at a distance from Rome, a kindred art seemed to be evolving; at Palmyra and in the Fayum the Roman form came in contact with the unchanging East — as Greek forms had done at the foot of the Pamir highland. Doubtless this Roman form had grown more than vulnerable; Rome did not need Byzantium to bid her forget the art of Trajan. The basic elements of the Arch of Constantine, his colossal statue, are already in a style opposed to what we call the Roman style. What was petrifying Roman figures was not yet Christianity, but the creeping paralysis of Rome herself. The Caesarian gesture was dead, and now

GILT GLASS (CA. 320)

it was no longer a question of discovering what new gesture was to replace it; but what artist was to animate immobility.

We have seen the East reconquering Palmyra. And now Islam crushed out these tentatives which were for painting what Palmyra was to sculpture — the beginnings of an obscure art which might have sponsored more of the Christian faith than did the catacombs: the art of the Fayum.

The Fayum, too, is a cemetery in which the great are mingled with the humble. Its artisans cared nothing for art or for posterity, but buried their pictures with the corpses. We may disregard their ant-like industry, since our museums have gathered much that outdoes it. Like all collective and anonymous arts, Fayum art abides by a set programme: that of associating the individual face with death's distinctive presence.

The Fayum invented neither the portrait, which it got from Rome, nor its evocation of death, always familiar in Egypt. But the Roman portrait was the opposite of a funerary image; the figures in the Etruscan tombs had bespoken a different kind of eternity, and as death took possession of Rome, the marble portrait was, little by little, to change its nature. The painted portrait, too, had been painted "after life." (The little portraits on gilt glass often remind us of the photographs one sees on some French graves.) The Fayum figures, whoever the artisan that made them, always — unconsciously no doubt — aimed high; once more that oldest land of death, which clasps in

FRAGMENT OF ANTIQUE FRESCO

an equal embrace the living and the dead, was bidding the latter confer on mortal flesh an illusion of eternity.

Never, assuredly, had any great nation been so consistently and thoroughly deprived of style as were the Romans. By this I mean not merely that they did not invent their forms, but also that they never had the genius which enabled Iran and Japan to endow the forms they took over with permanence and quality. The taste of Augustan Rome (it is erroneous to say that the Victor Emmanuel monument which lords it in the Rome of to-day is not Roman in spirit) was on a par with that of our Second Empire; and its temperament very different from that suggested by the Museum of Antiquities at Naples.

A false impression that this museum gives a sort of cross-section of antique painting has played no small part in shaping our opinion of the art of ancient Rome. Yet suppose Monte Carlo were buried under ashes to-day and, two thousand years hence, excavations brought it back to light, the impression given of our Western painting would be queer indeed! The most recent excavations at Pompeii, revealing *in situ* its shop-signs and house-decorations, show that this painting is really a commercialization of styles whose place of origin was far from Pompeii. Those crude human figures *à la* Magnasco (which remind us of our caricatural drawings) would probably, could they be compared with the superficial yet brilliant art we glimpse behind them, seem as tawdry as do copies of Timomachus when confronted with the originals — or as are the *Monna Lisas* on our calendars.

One major Roman work of art is extant, whose calligraphy, if not that of a master, is an artist's, and which casts into the shade the banal craftsmanship of the big figures that have been dug up, no less than the charming craftsmanship of the small ones; this is the ensemble of the "Villa of the Mysteries."

Some sanguines especially (whether mural or done on marble) vouch for a will to style which there is no mistaking. One is puzzled at first by the relation between the figures and the red background, which seemingly is that of the figures supplied to order by the house-decorator (quite different from those of a decorative style properly so called). Doubtless antique statues, painted and wax-polished, harmonized with such a setting; or perhaps this is an attempt at that escape from reality more effectively achieved by the gold backgrounds of the Middle Ages and the black backgrounds of Goya's aquatints. Here technique, style and spirit tend to put a distance between the spectator and the scene portrayed; we are, in fact, looking at a stage performance from which the spectator is as much separated as from a scene portrayed in sculpture. Moreover this art is affiliated to sculpture, despite obvious differences. True, neither the naked

POMPEII, VILLA OF THE MYSTERIES (CA. 50 B.C.). TERRIFIED WOMAN

women, nor that *Terrified Woman* who seems to be casting her veil adrift on the wind, resemble Roman statues; yet their *spaceless* masses, while not imitating bas-reliefs (the value of the background, equal at least to that of the figures, rules this out), vie with them. We hesitate to use the word "masses"; for us a mass always exists in Space. If we compare these figures to Piero della Francesca's, for instance, we are struck by the fact that they have no weight; the ground is their limit, not their base. To give them, if not relief — at which the artist does not aim — or a third dimension — of which he is ignorant — at least an accent other than that of two-dimensional painting

POMPEII, VILLA OF THE MYSTERIES. UNVEILING OF THE PHALLUS

(we need only picture how a Romanesque or Persian artist would have "adapted" this scene), the painter has recourse sometimes to a schematized lay-out, at once "Ingresque" and rudimentary, as in the kneeling figure bending above the veil that hides the phallus (curiously akin to the amusing parodies of Ingres that Cézanne painted at Le Jas de Bouffan), and sometimes to sophisticated drawing, at a very far remove from the trivial denizens of the Naples Museum, and the woman of the *Visitation*. Undoubtedly these figures suggest (and they are almost alone in suggesting) what Roman painting actually was.

POMPEII, VILLA OF THE MYSTERIES.　THE VISITATION (DETAIL)

Rome stood for that alone which *is*. How surprising is this huge depiction of the Dionysiac "Mysteries" to those for whom the terms "Mystery" and "Dionysus" have a meaning! And, if the gulf between the Roman portrait and those which followed it is so great, the reason is that Rome had no progeniture in any field; her mysteries were unveiled, like symbols, on bare walls, and her portraits were no more than "artistic" photographs. Even when Rome had mastered their technique she put no soul into them; for she had none. A dogged continuity, she had; but so have the sciences. Her portraiture, to which Rome attached so much importance, was that of faces separated from the universe. What efforts she expended in her paintings, realistic mosaics, gilt-glass portraits, to body forth the individual personality! And yet, despite all these efforts, that personality had no *value*. When, after having been the idiosyncratic face of the leader or the conqueror, the portrait came to be that of the ordinary citizen, it still fastened only on idiosyncrasies, while endowing them as best it could with a tawdry dignity. The innumerable busts that clutter up Italian galleries differ from or resemble each other like numbers on a catalogue, not like living men. Once it was discovered, first in the Fayum, then in the West, that a face means more than the sum of its features, Roman painting and sculpture passed away. A Roman face could no more be the intimation of a soul or the incarnation of a god than a Roman figure could convey its presence in Space or in the cosmos; empires, in art, are but feeble substitutes for a cosmos.

Nevertheless pagan Rome showed an unflinching fidelity to the principles on which her art was founded. It was by means of style that the Egypt of the Pharaohs had given life to its fantastic figures; Rome took them to pieces and put them together again, making with a realistic jackal's head placed on a realistic man's body, or a lioness's head on a woman's body, ingenious and effective *collages*. But Egypt had been style incarnate, and her age-long grappling with those very forms in which style was most conspicuously lacking is one of the most significant episodes in the whole history of art.

The Fayum portraits were painted on little wooden tablets which the shroud held to the corpse's face. Their art is not, whatever has been said, that of the masks of Antinoë, for the relations between the colours, the *matière*, sometimes too the brush-strokes, play a decisive part; but both alike are expressions of the same impulse, that which gave rise to the figures painted on the bottoms of the sarcophagi. These had long been more significant than the covers. Lacking relief, they came under the category of painting; while the carving on the exterior of the sarcophagus stood in the same relation to sculpture as does modern furniture-decoration. If sometimes we take a wrong view of them this is only in cases where the effigy has lost its colour. These covers, when, deserting the Egyptian tradition, they replace it with the tawdriness of the

third century, seem "cheap" to a degree! One would think that all the Mediterranean gods had forgathered in the oases, there to lay to rest a motley company of gilt and sugar-candy figurines, in the "pink style" of the sweetmeat booths at our country fairs! Yet these same figures, when portrayed in the flat on the bottom of the coffin, have a very different style. We know well how the process of decay can enrich even the tawdriest colours, and perhaps we would do best not to conjure up what they looked like when freshly painted; still they, anyhow, have nothing in common with the Baroque vulgarities of our fairs, nor are they a retrogression, for Egypt had never used them. Those patches of salmon-pink and ashen blue, rimmed or traversed by black lines, in a curiously restless, consciously ornate calligraphy, here acquire a significance other than the same colours when lacquered and figuring on the gilt "papier-mâché" surface of the lids. There is no mistaking their accent; if it be that of creations doomed to perish, it is none the less that of creations. We seem to feel in them Egypt's last effort in her death-throes to drag down with her into that Kingdom of the Dead which she has served so faithfully, all that she still can call her own from the Euphrates to the Tiber.

But these sarcophagus paintings are mere *signs* — dramatic signs, perhaps, but signs none the less. Though, instead of a rendering of the likeness of the dead person by a constantly heightened stylization, they have the febrililty of the "abstractions" of the Syrian East, this is abstraction none the less. Whereas the Fayum portraits we are now considering are *not* abstract; in them the living being is

something more than so much raw material, indicated by a few fixed signs, awaiting the final touch of Death.

Essentially, they are Roman portraits (no more than that, when the artist scamps his work), and at first they have the over-facile harmony, the unambitious art of these. Whenever it aspired to being a work of art, the Roman portrait became sculpture; the paintings were but effigies. They were products of a technique, like the common run of photographs to-day. But, whereas the Romans intended their portraits of this kind to be effigies, what now was wanted was to supersede these. And the new portrait did not try to compete with these effigies, but with the Roman bust. This, after "discovering" the individual, had changed him into a Roman; now he was to be changed into a dead man — not into a corpse, but into something which was only just beginning to be called a "soul."

Several styles had been bound up with the feeling of death, but a feeling that involved awareness. In Fayum art this feeling was seeking for its form, which Rome had withdrawn from it, and never replaced. And in the process of transforming the Latin portrait, the new art discovered that something had been amputated, so to speak, and applied itself to restoring the contact with the other world that had been lost. What did

FAYUM PORTRAIT (ROMAN PERIOD)

it seek to impart to those portraits sometimes painted on the winding-sheet itself? The eternal face of death. The Egypt of the Pharaohs had ensured its eternity by a style which translated all forms into a hieratic language; indeed such a style was inseparable from a religion capable of permeating the whole of life. Now, however, the positive sense of death organized for an after-life was being replaced by its negative: the sense of *that which is not life*, of that grey limbo to which gods, evil spirits and the dead had long been relegated indiscriminately.

This is why Christian art allied itself with these portraits in so far as Christianity was a repudiation of the pagan world, and why it broke with them once it became an affirmation. Man has oftener sponsored an after-life he thinks he knows, than one he knows he does not know.

From that limbo come some of the methods of expression which strikingly accord with modern sensibility. Schematic structure, to begin with; trivial details were ruled out, as being accessories either of realism (and realism could express the living man or the corpse, but not the dead), or of a triumphant idealization incompatible with bereavement. Also, the usage of a range of colour often passing from white to brown

DERAIN. DRAWING

by way of various ochres, a colour-scheme Derain rediscovered, as well as a style of portraiture near enough to that of the Fayum to show clearly both what they have in common and what separates them. Then — and this struck deeper than our modern, expert "disintegrations" — the use of pure, unblended colour. Figures, in which the white-and-ocre harmony is not employed, keep to the Syrian gamut, the pinks and blues of Dura-Europos, deepening them sometimes to aubergine purple, or purplish-red. These colours persisted in Coptic art, even when (deliberately, it would seem) it set to reducing the pensive gravity of Fayum art, and the emotionalism of the sarcophagus paintings, to geometry. Lastly, in studying the work, or anyhow the masterpieces of these

craftsmen, we are struck by the remarkable stiffness of the figures; and this seems to owe less to the rigidity of the dead body than to their disdain for the febrile agitation of the living. The bodies are motionless, but so is eternity; not without reason had Egypt selected basalt as the material for her statues. No doubt this stiffness is partly due to clumsiness, but it derives also from the "frontalism" of Egyptian statuary; indeed it is less a matter of rigidity than of the schematization, mentioned above, which is one of the few equivalents in painting (prior to Romanesque painting) of the great anti-humanistic types of sculpture.

The painted tablets of Fayum are different from the ornamental art of Palmyra, and their broad planes owe nothing to the pre-Byzantine, perhaps Parthian, accents of the Syrian desert. But they are akin, vaguely albeit, to sculpture; they reject alike the heritage of the phalanx and that of the legion (despite Palmyra's military associations), and likewise seek to go beyond imitation in their likenesses. Also this art knows all about the gaze, a gaze that is not the expression of a fleeting moment, nor yet that hypnotic stare of the Byzantines, but often has in it a still, small glow of a life eternal, spanning the gulf between this world and the world to come.

FAYUM PORTRAIT (DETAIL)

Did this art die of having worked in the service of death? True, it was not the first art to do this, but it was the first to work solely for the tomb. Though the religious sentiment finds in solitude a refuge, solitude does not favour its development; it is nourished by communion, to which the church is more propitious than the cemetery. This indeed was Christian Rome's vocation, and so evident is it, that her art found in the mosaic its natural method of expression, that all mosaics previous to the "Decadence" strike us as wholly decorative. Popular as was the miniature (primarily because, being incorporated in a manuscript, it was easily transportable), it soon led up to the mosaic, in which, during the fourth century, enamel came to replace marble, and which transcended the miniature as, at a later period, Romanesque tympana were to transcend it. The apse of St Pudentiana, that of Sts. Cosmas and Damian, are no mere enlargements of miniatures but exist in their own right. Meanwhile the fresco was the

ANTIOCH (Vth CENT.). A SEASON

poor man's mosaic; but if the mosaic (which led up to the stained-glass window) was for so long the most favoured means of expression of Christian art, this was not because of its glittering parade of affluence, but owing to its aptitude for the suggestion of the divine.

Thus there is no need to attribute to its technical traditions the hieratic quality of the Christian figures. Even the *Seasons* at Antioch which, while belonging

ROMAN MOSAIC

to pagan art, show strong Eastern influences, are hieratic, and the drawing of some pagan mosaics had been as free as that of Matisse. It is easy to picture, growing up around the St Pudentiana apse, a whole school no farther from Assisi than from Byzantium. Did it ever exist? Rome's irremediable decline was unlikely to foster a revival of the majestic. Its new expression was to become manifest in the apse of St Cosmas. And now the Christ who had replaced the Good Shepherd was himself replaced by the Christ of Judgement Day. History had moved across to Byzantium.

Yet how vigorously Rome defended herself! The spirit of St Cosmas is that of the Old Testament, but its monumental drawing was somewhat different from that which was being perfected on the Bosphorus. This work is little known because not only its texture, but also, and especially, its dimensions fare so badly in reproduction. But while St Pudentiana sets us dreaming of Assisi, here we have intimations of the Carmine; who else was to achieve those mighty masses, that dramatic architecture, before Masaccio?

Within four centuries the face of Europe had been transformed, and with it had changed the function of painting, the world whose expression painting claimed as its domain. For early Christendom the Gospels had been inseparable from the sombre postscript given by St Paul; Christianity had meant not the incursion of love alone, but that of the voice of the Eternal, into a civilization in which all that survived of the Eternal was the aureole of the victorious general. Rome (as, probably, Greece before her) was unaware that forms and colours can express the tragic *by their own specific qualities;* in sculpture as in painting the various *Dying Gauls* express a tragedy only by illustrating it. The styles of Byzantium and the Middle Ages (and some later ones) have shown us that the tragic has its styles; but Antiquity did not know this. When its line did not tend towards idealization, it kept to an incorrigible puerility; — and how much of this was needed to make of Pasiphaë that figure in the Vatican Museum!

The colour, too, had remained that of an era,

PASIPHAE. ANTIQUE FRESCO

FRAGMENT OF THE APSE OF ST PUDENTIANA, ROME (402-417)

FRAGMENT OF THE APSE OF SAINTS COSMAS AND DAMIAN, ROME (CA. 530)

not reconciled, but anterior to the world's tragedy. The earliest Christian arts were international; but, in fact, the East had transmitted to Rome bright colours (and still was thriving on them) — the dominant hue of the Dura frescos is pink. The pinks and blues of the Santa Maria Antica frescos, though they do not express the spirit of Antiquity, convey its outward aspect, drained of what it had once expressed and incapable of expressing anything else; their *Crucifixion*, with its background of sombre violet attuned to the tragically emotive drawing of Christ's face, shows up like a hostile presence amongst those pale vestiges with which monks (hailing probably from Cappadocia) seemed to be trying to perpetuate, amidst the pines and wild roses of the Aventine, both a nostalgic memory of the ancient world and the glamour of Asia Minor. (Many outstanding works of Romanesque painting, the frescos of St Savin, for instance, were to show that their artists had no notion of the emotional and dramatic possibilities of colour in itself.) We may be sure it was not due to chance that the Catacomb artist so often used brown in his signs; but their simple pathos was inadequate to express the tragic sense of life.

Employing methods of portrayal which excluded realistic illusionism, Christian art, when it was led to substitute for this a surface which seemed trying to break loose from the wall — a paradoxical ambition subsequently realized triumphantly by the stained-glass window — and volumes which were not mere light-and-shade, set itself problems never raised before. From St Pudentiana onwards, colour in full awareness played a part no longer limited to dramatic expression. At St Cosmas it is the dark intensity of the recesses of the cupola that, balancing the heavy masses of the figures, frees them from the aspect of a bas-relief. The blues and whites of the ornamental compositions, the brown and gold which in San Apollinare Nuovo (at Ravenna) hark

APSE OF SAINTS COSMAS AND DAMIAN

back to the decorative tradition, belong to another domain of art. That of colour was explored in the little scenes at Santa Maria Maggiore; in St Pudentiana it had achieved its balance and its plainsong in monumental composition; at St Cosmas, abandoning simpler forms of harmony, it attained an orchestration based on contrasts that maintained and amplified it, as flying buttresses were to shore up, ever higher, the naves of the cathedrals. Surely El Greco felt a thrill of joy when he set eyes on the red of those clouds billowing round Christ against a background whose noontide blue darkens and deepens little by little into the profound blue of the Roman night. In this superb mosaic were intimations of a new art coming to birth, and history, when it now withdrew from Rome, forsook there the first great painter of the West.

DETAIL OF THE APSE

FRAGMENT OF THE APSE OF SAINTS COSMAS AND DAMIAN.   CHRIST

SECOND STUDY

Addendum to the comments on art as a direct expression of the instinct.

CELTIC COIN (JERSEY)

ONCE so light-heartedly applied to the mediaeval sculptors, the theory that art can be a direct expression of the instinct (rendered more complex nowadays by being named "the unconscious") has now shifted its field of activity to so-called retrograde art, whether popular or "barbaric." A lesson may perhaps be drawn from the fact that this theory fits so badly a "barbaric" art which will soon conspicuously be coming to the fore and whose evolution we know better than that of the

STATER OF PHILIP II OF MACEDONIA

fetishes : the art of Celtic (often styled Gallic) coins. Their character and dimensions seemed once to put them outside the pale of art ; but at last photographic enlargement has won them a place in it. Can so distinctive a style have emerged merely as a sort of by-product in the process of minting the coins ? Though not yet in a position to compile its history, we know the genealogy of several of its figures. And we see them combining purposive activity and what looks like instinct with a rugged force far to seek in any early Christian arts ; indeed we feel that the spirit of ancient Gaul finds a more direct expression in this vehemence than in the few effigies of its "hammer gods" that have survived, or even in the figures of Roquepertuse and Antremont. There is no trace of religious influence, and these forms seem to owe to the metal in which they are struck, sometimes gold, that dignity combined with preciosity which the nomads' plaques owed to the fact of their adorning their battle-harness, and Viking carvings to their use as figureheads. Doubtless the conditions under which the art of numismatics worked were more restricted, but not more so than those imposed on the religious art of the ancient East ; indeed we may liken the evolution of these forms ranging from England to Transylvania with that of the forms of the Sumerian, even the Egyptian gods.

Involved as is their filiation, we can trace the metamorphosis they imposed, over several centuries, on the coins of classical Antiquity. The change from representation to the sign, to begin with ; and, likewise, from humanist expression to barbarian expression, or the abstract. Not that this meant a steady retrogression towards the sign, for the sign is not invariably their final expression ; it is only the form of their death. This art does not move on from the stater of Philip to the ideogram of the tribe of the

VELIOCASSES

Veliocasses by way of the gold coin of the Osismii of Armorica; it follows divergent paths, ending up with the two last named, just as Roman art made its way from the Capitol to the most degenerate signs the West has known, *but also* to Romanesque art; to the most effete signs of Arabia, *but also* to Byzantine art.

Here, as elsewhere, the sign is but a residue. It reappears from time to time, especially when its function changes — as when it does duty for a signature, rather than for the forms it has replaced. The ideogram of the Veliocasses, in any case, is simply a breaking up of the best Armorican figures, which seemed at first to aim at taking to pieces their classical prototypes with a view to recombining them into new patterns. The ideogram, however, does not show a face at all: only two tresses, a

OSISMII (ARMORICA)

headband, a nose, an eye. Indeed, did we not know its origin, we could not decipher it; the ear, for instance, has become a sun!

Doubtless, the influence of glyptics plays some part in this art; but by no means a decisive part. Once we become familiar with these figures, they lose the qualities which seem to assimilate them to Sumerian seals or engraved stones, and we soon see that their makers were as diverse in outlook as were the Romanesque sculptors. In most heads the treatment of the masses revives that of the Second Iron Age, less as a calligraphy than as an ineradicable "language." (Similarly, we see an angularity, more or less pronounced, persisting through so many types of Chinese art.) The makers of these

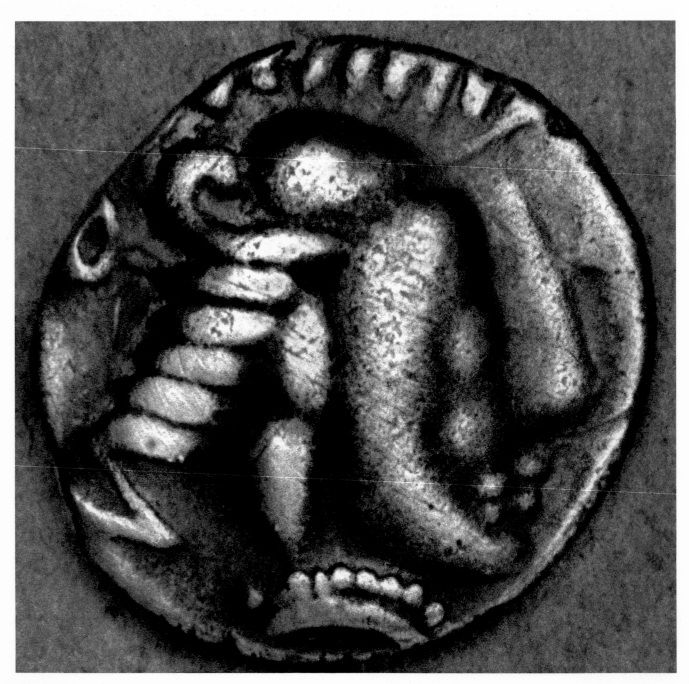

GALLIC "IMITATION" OF A RHODA COIN

"EYE COIN"

coins composed the profile with small separately modelled, then agglomerated, units ; this *pastillage* (as ceramists call it) differed from the Sumerian, and permitted, as in the tresses on the coins "imitating" those of Rhoda in Catalonia, the utmost freedom of execution.

Later, the relief became less pronounced, but the drawing still derived from binding masses with thick outlines — the effect being that of a mosaic in low relief. The faces on the coins of the Parisii look as if they were chalked in on a dark background, but, here too, the outlines enclosed masses like those of the earlier profiles. These masses can easily be reconstituted ; the two balls at the extremities of the spur-like mouth belong to them. Sometimes, when attrition or may be the coin-moulder himself, has flattened the planes building up the face, which, run together, acquire a swirling movement reminiscent of Baroque.

CARNUTES

PARISII

CORIOSOLITES

At its opposite pole this art raises traditionally sunken passages into relief, but without losing the compelling unity of the masses characteristic of Celtic numismatic art. We have only vestiges here to whet our imaginations, and much research-work will be needed before our theories become authenticated facts; yet surely that first artist who, moving beyond the harmony of forms to which that coin of the Osismii bears admirable witness, devised that of the coin of the Coriosolites, was what we call to-day a Master. Hair, nose, lips, are still in relief, but now the eyelids too, which formerly were hollows, are ridges; while the eye has become a hollow, whereas formerly it was in relief. Most noteworthy of all, the cheek (almost always the largest salient) is now an almost flat plane, less protruding than the forehead.

The bottom of the face from the chin downwards has become purely abstract, and another abstract passage joins the nose with what began as a lock of hair. Did the Gallic artists, one wonders, transform Mediterranean coins because they did not understand their meaning, or was it because their meaning did not interest them? They replace a charioteer's cloak billowing on the wind, by a buckler, partly no doubt because the cloak has been effaced on the original, but also because they prefer the buckler; next, they replace the buckler by a winged figure. When they substitute a sun for an ear, need we assume they failed to notice that a head has ears? Likewise that man-headed horse, so widespread at the time, is not blunder of interpretation. Rarely has an artist displayed to better effect than on these small engraved surfaces, a happy gift of clothing the skeleton of his style with the living form that took his fancy. Thus the curved patch of a lion on Massalian coins became one of a squid; loosed from the neck, the pearl necklace of classical coins scattered into the little "pre-historic" blobs figuring on Armorican coins.

A detailed list of these mutations would be helpful, no doubt — but can we doubt what it would convey to us? From "degeneration" to "degeneration" the head of Hermes on the stater of Philip II of Macedonia disintegrated; but it so happened that this disintegration resulted in — a lion's head.

TRANSYLVANIA

A motif often found on the reverse of these coins is the winged horse. As regards the horse, civilized and barbaric races had more in common than as regarding Man; both Vercingetorix and Alexander were — amongst other things — cavalry generals. In Aquitania the horse became a geometrical figure, but freely and variously treated; sometimes its curve is regulated by the animal's hind foot and the head of its rider (who has replaced the wing), while the body of the latter and the horse's tail are straight lines and the mane is built up with the little "blobs" characteristic of this art. In the coin of the Lemovices, the horse is in keeping with its fantastic rider; we find it again amongst the Parisii, minus its rider and with wings, and here its form bursts asunder into

AQUITANIA

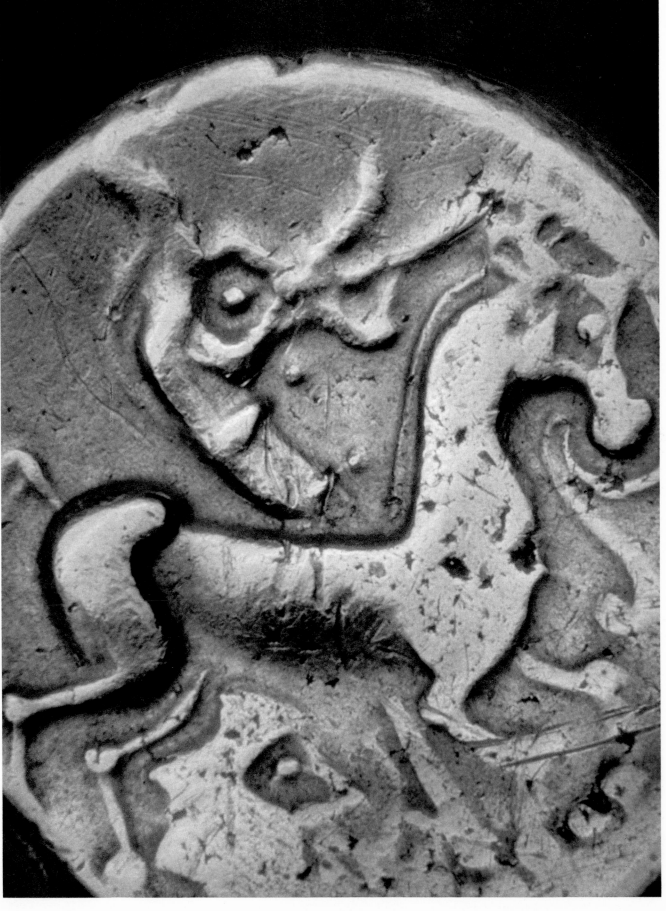

LEMOVICES (FRAGMENT)

PARISII (FRAGMENT)

arabesques — those of an almost purely ornamental art resembling that of Persian pottery.

But we have nothing of the East here. Nor of the Steppes. The art of the latter (sometimes akin to that of Altamira) shows us "armoured" animals closely locked in conflict; this interlocking, as obligatory as was the frontal posture in Egypt, musculature in Assyria, and freedom of movement in Greece, is here replaced by a tumultuous dispersal. Even when the Armorican coins lost their vigorous structure, and when in the Dordogne (home of the art of the caverns), the engravers seem harking back to some totemic boar, each line still looks like a split-off bone. Everywhere the horse "bursts asunder," as does the human face. The profile — most human of lines — was first to go; then came the turn of the hair. The various Celtic races in different parts of Europe treated the

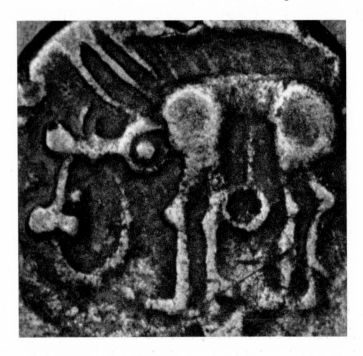

PETROCORII (DORDOGNE)

clean-shaven or bearded faces taken over from Hellas and Rome on greatly differing lines; but, from the beards in lumps of some British coins, to the chipped beards of most of the "imitations" of Philip's stater, and the foliated beards of the Armoricans, always the artist tried to re-assemble the human face in terms of rules he himself had framed. Until he succeeded in so doing — or the face disappeared altogether.

In this latter case, the result was a startling modernism. The engraver was no less obsessed by the circular surface he was about to slash with vehement lines, than is a modern artist by the rectangle of his canvas. The forms of the Atrebates, whose abstract patterns were still governed by a feeling for movement akin to that of André Masson, were replaced in England and the Somme region by static compositions;

static, yet in their lay-out almost frenzied — which is all the more surprising in that the art of coin-making is not an art of solitude (but neither, for that matter, is Negro art). Here the numismatist may see merely signs; not so the sculptor. No longer have we here an eye and there a nose sprinkled on the surface; instead, we have that menacing sickle, and, below, a concave ring balancing the convex boss. For one alleged to be the tool of instinct, this art is singularly purposive!

In those so-called "eye coins" — in which it would seem that the eye of the original face has invaded the whole surface — are we to attribute it to incredible clumsiness, a retrogression to the verge of infantilism, that the die-makers (who engraved the traditional horse on the reverse) ended up by enclosing, *within the eye*, the abstract elements of the former profile? The eye itself has given place to a triangle. These artists certainly did not forget that a man's nose is not inside his eye; nor did they suppose that by this device they were expressing more vigorously the characteristics of a face; no, they decided that a face is a means to a composition in relief, which is governed by *its own laws*.

Shall we say that into these coins, as into certain fetishes, there enters *an element* of instinctive expression? But this there is in Rembrandt, in Michelangelo, in the metopes of the Parthenon. It used actually to be asserted that these coins, and likewise the fetishes, were the expression of untrammelled instinct, and on a par with the drawings of a child or a madman. But neither purposiveness nor conscious thought is absent in a madman's drawing; as for children's water-colour sketches, if, after the first lucky hits, they become "organized," they come to nothing. Since it is obviously not the

SOMME DISTRICT

case that the best sculptor of some terrifying god is the most terror-stricken member of the tribe, what is it that gives his style its power? Either he is copying previous forms (in which case it is their inventor who concerns us), or else he is inventing them. Why then does he keep to so rigorous a style? Does mere chance account for the Polynesians' never having carved a single "Negro" statue? Is this because the Polynesian soil makes Polynesian art sprout automatically, like the breadfruit-trees? And "barbarian" soil, barbarian coins? If so, why are they not more like each other? How marvellous must be the "unconscious" of New Ireland, which gives rise to fetishes as complicated as games of patience; and that of the Osismii, which sets up a system of bars and "blobs" against volumes bound in by arabesques, and amplifies its conquests, coin by coin, till they link up with the compositions of 1950! What was gained by heaping scorn on Taine's theories, if only to imitate them tamely when barbaric art was in question? For such an "unconscious" would be no longer individual, but racial or local; and its total freedom would gradually shade off into sheer determinism...

Quite obviously consciousness must play a smaller part in the *life* of a designer of Armorican coins or that of a maker of fetishes than in that of a Pheidias; but does it necessarily play a proportionately smaller part in his *art*? Clearly the consciousness of an artist does not mean a gift for making theories. We have mentioned that the kings of the Balubas refrained from having their effigies made, when there were no "good sculptors" available. What, then, were these "good sculptors"? However large the share of instinct in the art of a savage race, it is rarely that this instinct does not take its fulcrum, as in our art, on some previous work. To discern the limits of instinct in a Baluba craftsman, a graver of Armorican coins, a mediaeval artist, a Douanier Rousseau, we need only to review their works in their chronological order. There are elements of instinct, chance and play in the little Sumerian terracottas, as in the black Lagash stone figurines; but not the same elements. Undoubtedly a great artist gives rein to his instinct — but only after he has mastered it; that illusion of the omnipotence of instinct in art arose with the rediscovery of Gothic, as it arises whenever the lead is taken by an art of forms for which neither an aesthetic of beauty, nor any theory of the imitation of nature, can account.

THIRD STUDY

Addendum to "the metamorphosis of forms of art" (in continuation of the analyses of the art of El Greco and that of Tintoretto, with reference to the metamorphosis of living forms).

IT WELL may be that there exists no more striking example of the annexation of one system of forms by another, than the transformation of Caravaggio's red-and-black pictures into the art of Georges de Latour.

The unstable fame of Caravaggio was at its zenith when Latour came to know his art — which was to affect the whole of Western Europe. If an influence is to be assessed in borrowings of themes and colours, rarely have we seen an influence so strong as this. Latour took over from him his card-players, his musicians, his mirror, his Magdalen, his St Francis, his Crowning with Thorns (which became the "Christ of Pity"), his St Jerome; his association of dark backgrounds with red drapery, sometimes even his particular shade of red; and likewise he employed a very similar lighting — yet, none the less, achieved an art almost diametrically opposed to Caravaggio's.

The explanation is that the underlying principles of Latour's art were entirely different and he used what he took over *for other ends*.

In Caravaggio we have a "nonconformist" more earnest than ever was Cellini; indeed his realism was, for him, a sort of gospel. It was his conviction that he could impart more veracity to New Testament figures by giving them the faces of his friends than by idealizing them. Already Gothic painting and sculpture had discovered how effective the portrayal of the living individual's face could be, and Caravaggio's figures are (no doubt as he intended) never of the accepted religious types. When sometimes he slips up — as when in his *Descent from the Cross* he gives the man who is holding up Christ's body the face of some old working-man — this is because he is not ruling out emotional "abstraction" (as Gothic art ruled out the Romanesque "abstraction"), but idealization, and merely individualizing figures was not enough to banish it. The

Gothics had the secret of a very different power of communication. We have only to compare his figures with Latour's St Joseph, and, looking but a little ahead, Rembrandt's "Saints." Caravaggio thought to break away both from idealization and Italian Baroque, but he did not break with either as thoroughly as he supposed. The characters in his big canvases gesticulate; thus, in the *Descent* the uplifted arms of the woman on the right seem alien to the picture (we need only cover them to see this); in the *Vocation* St Matthew is hardly in the same style as the gamblers; St Anne's face in the *Madonna*

CARAVAGGIO.   DESCENT FROM THE CROSS (DETAIL)

CARAVAGGIO. DESCENT FROM THE CROSS

THE MADONNA OF THE OSTLERS (THE VIRGIN)

of the Ostlers, while not a portrait, is at once a replica of the Madonna's face aged by the painter's imagination, and a traditional Italian face, treated "realistically."

His art, indeed, is something of a medley. It seems to anticipate Courbet in its handling of colour, sumptuous and thickly put on, but lacking distinctive touches; to aspire, far more than Courbet's, to a photographic realism, never in practice to be achieved; and also to aim at both that still life realism whose offspring was the chromo, and a fighting realism, a passionate — almost, perhaps, Dostoevskian — counterblast to that Baroque idealization whose profounder implications Caravaggio rejected, but which he never actually abandoned. It was his feeling for the monumental style that enabled him to create some magnificently simplified figures, incompatible though these were with his realism, with what remained of the Baroque in his make-up, and often with his lighting; for the lighting alone seemed to him capable of giving his realism that grandeur which meant so much to him. In his art persisted a very Italian strain of lyricism, grandiose yet turbid, which is illustrated by his *David* (Goliath's head is said to be a self-portrait), and was to come out more strongly in his immediate followers, finding brilliant expression in Manfredi. And in some of his ostensibly realistic works (the *Madonna of the Ostlers* is one of them) we find an idealization of the

THE MADONNA OF THE OSTLERS (ST ANNE)

individual as a "character," which he inherited from Mantegna's old women, and which, though typically Italian, reappeared in most of his Northern imitators. He died at the age of forty-six. Had he lived, would he have integrated his art? It was left to Rembrandt to discover that lighting which, wresting humble figures from the darkness, invests them with eternity.

Less than towards Latour, this art pointed the way towards Ribera. A more drastic but less individualizing realism, a discreeter use of gesture, a less complex but surer handling of dark colours, a fervid austerity seconded by well-controlled lighting — all these gave Ribera's art the unity his master had perhaps disdained. And we need only look at Latour after Ribera to see how allergic is the former's genius to Caravaggio's.

Latour never gesticulates. In an age of frenzied agitation he avoids movement. We do not even pause to wonder if he was capable of rendering it well or not ; for he simply leaves it out. There is nothing of Ribera's histrionics in his art, which, if theatrical,

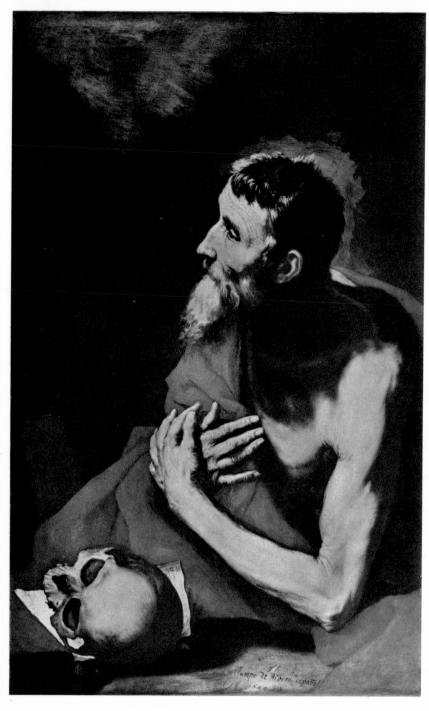

RIBERA. ST JEROME IN PRAYER

partakes rather of the Mystery Play, or the slow rhythms of a rite. It is unlikely that he knew Piero della Francesca. But the same devotion to style gives his figures that immobility, timeless rather than primitive, which we find in the Nouans *Pietà,* in Uccello, sometimes in Giotto. That, too, of Olympia. Whereas in the Baroque gesture the arms are usually spread out far from the body, the gestures in Latour's art bring them in towards the body, like those expressing love or an uprush of tense emotion. Rarely do the elbows of his figures quit the torso, nor are the fingers of an outstretched hand (in the *St Sebastian,* for instance) extended. And the figures placed on the margin of a group seem drawn towards its centre as potently as those in a Baroque group break away from it.

We might think to see in this the influence of sculpture ; but the sculpture of his day gesticulated like the painting. And Latour's figures, while their effect of weight exceeds that made by Persian "verticality," are redeemed from heaviness by a curious translucency (imperfectly brought out in black-and-white reproduction). Shall we say there is a secret in Latour ?

Every great artist has his "secret," which is none other than the particular method by which his genius usually expresses itself. Latour is a colourist of a very special order ;

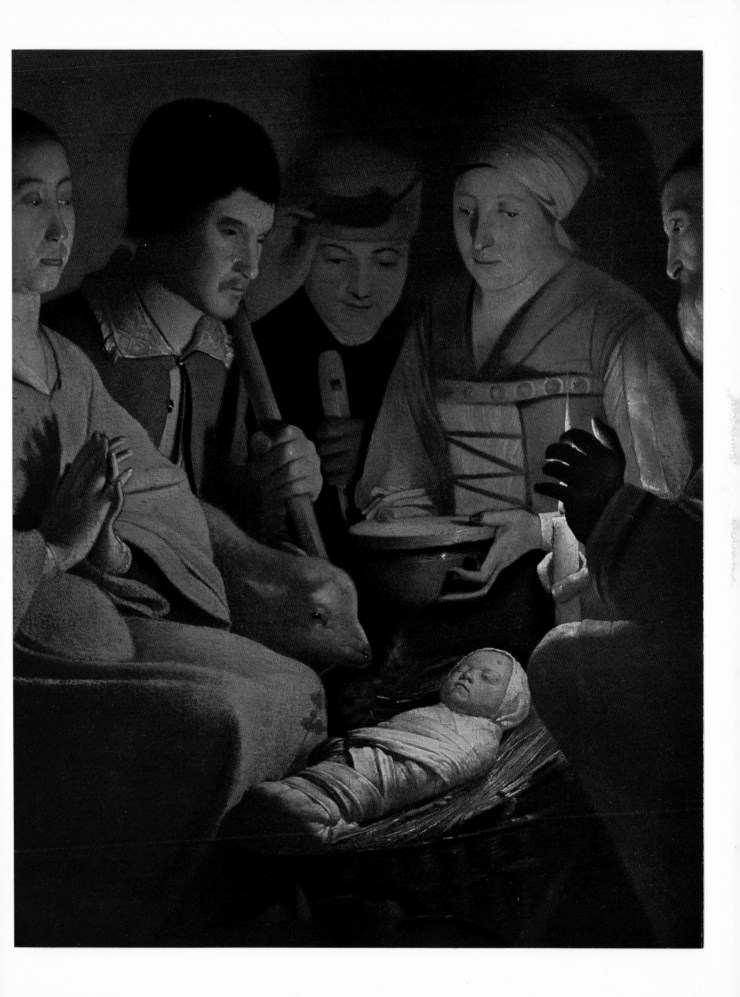

in his work colour is never subordinated to the model, and his palette seems always built up around *red*. From red he modulates to grey, from red to yellow ochre, from red to brown or black; only one of his canvases is really multi-coloured. On the face of it this palette is identical with Caravaggio's in his various *St Jeromes* and *St John the Baptists*. Yet who could ascribe Latour's *Prisoner* to the painter of the *St Jerome* in the Galleria Borghese?

An obvious point of contact is to be found, no doubt, in the gamblers in the *Vocation of St Matthew,* whose novelty drew crowds to see them in the French Church at Rome. But there were similar points of contact in pictures whose execution differs greatly from this fresco's. Resembling that of the Flemish artists, Caravaggio's colour is rich and lavish; whereas Latour's is almost transparent. The lighting remedies the opacity of the former, and its glow the transparence of the latter. Caravaggio aims at an effect of relief (a relief less sculptural than modern) and uses a treacly pigment that he models; Latour, even when he indulges in thickly laid on colour, as in his *St Joseph the Carpenter* — a work exceptional in his output and, strangely enough,

CARAVAGGIO. THE VOCATION OF ST MATTHEW (FRAGMENT)

recalling to us Cousin's *Eva Prima Pandora* — does not aim at imparting relief ; he shuns it. Only a genius like his could work the miracle of conjuring up a Caravaggio become translucent. His "secret" was that of rendering, in a portrayal seemingly naturalistic, certain volumes as though they were surfaces — *in flat planes.*

Hence his nearness to the art of to-day (and to Giotto), and his complete divergence from Caravaggio. Caravaggio was a firm believer in "the real," and the emotional tension of his style, at its best, comes from the fact that, while his talent bade him cling to this realism, his genius urged him to break free from it. The function of his shadowy backgrounds is to implement his light ; of his light to implement that on which it falls ; and that on which it falls to become more real than reality, to stand out more prominently, whether emphasizing character or dramatic situations. Beginning by still lifes in which an apple tried to be rounder than a sphere, he achieved a form of painting standing often in much the same relation to what went before it as high relief does to low relief. Latour's discovery, on the other hand, was that of a surface which,

CARAVAGGIO. FRUIT AND FOLIAGE

while not excluding three-dimensional volume, suggests it, instead of portraying it; which presents a mass *that does not turn upon itself*. And the traditional candle is used only to justify it. Illustrations are the woman painted side-face in *The Cheat*, the women in *St Peter's Denial*, the woman on the left in the *New-born Babe*, the man with the moustache in *The Adoration*, the book and garment in the Louvre *St Jerome*, the hat in the Stockholm *St Jerome*, the face and arm of the Grenoble *St Jerome*, the women in the background of *St Sebastian*.

The same applies to the faces of the various children holding candles; those in Detroit, in the *Education of the Virgin*, and the *Angel Appearing to St Peter*; likewise to the receding, yet almost flat, surfaces of the two *Magdalens*. We find the same procedure in the child Christ in *St Joseph the Carpenter* — here it is enough to cover up the face (over-much cleaned) to change the whole style of the picture — and it is present almost everywhere in *The Prisoner*, where the red band below is a wholly abstract passage. Caravaggio paints figures in the middle distance (for which he has no liking) just like the foreground figures; whereas Latour paints them, even if only a little in retreat, quite differently, sketch-wise and — deliberately — side-face,

GEORGES DE LATOUR. THE CHEAT

and without relief. The grey face of the man with the stick in *The Adoration of the Shepherds,* immediately on the right of the Virgin and above the Child (who might well have been drawn by Fouquet), shows how effectively he can cut free from the real, and how he goes about it.

These flat passages adjusted to the three-dimensional volumes (as had been done, though by other methods, by Giotto and Piero della Francesca, and was, later, to be done by Cézanne) indicate a very different approach from that of Caravaggio. We can easily imagine a copy *à la* Cézanne, not to say Cubist, of *The Prisoner,* but not one of the *Descent from the Cross.* An amazing art — especially when we consider the part the lighting plays in it ; for it. is his lighting that enables Latour to create planes without relief or modelling.

Some have said that, like those contemporaries of his who specialized in night-pieces, Latour had worked out a theory of light. This is wrong. Fascinating as are his light effects, they are not scientifically correct ; as we should promptly see did we reconstruct those scenes of his and photograph them.

It is common knowledge that torches figure often in his pictures ; but has a torch ever diffused that even glow which shows up volumes and does not bring out accents ? The bodies in *St Sebastian* cast shadows, but only those the painter wants of them ; thus there is no shadow in the foreground of *The Prisoner* which does not serve his turn. Let us not forget that Caravaggio's lighting usually comes from a stray beam of sunshine, often the ray piercing one of those peep-holes which were his speciality. It wrests his figures from a sombre background, and emphasizes their

features. Latour's pale flames serve to unite his figures; his candle is the source of a diffused light (despite the sharpness of his planes), and this light, far from being realistic, is *timeless,* as is Rembrandt's. Great as is the difference between Rembrandt's genius and Latour's, there is much in common in their poetic vision. Neither set out to copy the effects of light; rather, each evoked them with just sufficient accuracy to secure the spectator's assent, that credibility which, visionaries though they were, seemed to them indispensable.

Balzac made a similar discovery when he found that he could "put across" the fantastic most tellingly by drawing largely on the real. Moreover, what Latour takes from the real is often perceived with an amazing keenness; the candlelight glowing through the fingers of the child Jesus in *The Carpenter* is a case in point. But his light is not, like Caravaggio's, a means for bringing out relief, nor, like Honthorst's, a means to picturesque effect; it creates a harmony in which the real becomes the setting of some "great good place" of tranquil meditation.

Moreover, the methods he uses to this end are exclusively those of painting. But when a great painter is a poet the methods of his poetry are, by the same token, those of his painting. This light "that never was" calls forth relations between forms which likewise are not wholly real. The difference between Latour's daylight pictures and his night scenes is far greater than would seem at first sight, even when the colours are akin, and even when these works are almost replicas, as in the case of the Stockholm and the Grenoble *St Jeromes*. The difference, it may be said, lies merely in the special lighting of the night-pieces. But Latour's small sources of illumination do more than merely implement the lighting of the picture. The lighting of Caravaggio and his school tends, as I have said, to bring out figures in full relief ("in the round"), and to withdraw them from a shadowy background.

But Latour does not paint shadowy backgrounds; he paints night itself — that darkness mantling the world and that serenity in which, since the dawn of time, men have found their respite from the mystery of things. His figures are not withdrawn from it; rather, they are its very emanation. Sometimes we find it taking form in a little girl whom he calls an angel, and elsewhere in the guise of women, or even in a glow of torches or small lamps which does not ruffle its repose. And the whole world seems bathed in that limitless night brooding on sleeping hosts of long-ago, whence the lantern of the night-patrol called forth, step by quiet step, unmoving forms. Slowly, in that crowded darkness, a small light kindles and reveals shepherds pressing around a Child, the Nativity whose wavering gleam will spread to the farthest corners of the earth. No other painter, not even Rembrandt, can so well suggest that vast, elemental stillness; Latour alone is the interpreter of the serene that dwells in the heart of darkness.

GENTILESCHI. SAN TIBURZIO

In his finest works he invents human forms attuned to that darkness. And his art culminates not in sculpture but in the statue. That the women in *St Sebastian Bewailed by St Irene* and *The Prisoner* look like nightbound statues, is due not to their density or weight, but to their immobility — that of apparitions of the antique world; they do not come from afar, but have arisen from the slumbering earth, each a Pallas of compassion.

This is why, though he took over so much from Caravaggio, he took nothing of that in which each, after his own fashion, affirmed his genius. It was no more difficult then than it is now to distinguish the different elements which met, rather than intermingled, in Caravaggio's pictures. His so-called monumental figures (which, however, do not make us think of statuary) ill accord with his realistic figures; one feels, indeed, that an artist more mindful than he of harmony might well have thought up figures akin to those monumental figures, grouping around them others of the same style. (The *Death of the Virgin,* if "rectified," could well belong to an art very close to that of the Nouans *Pietà.*) Caravaggio's more faithful disciples, however, while retaining these figures, retained alongside them realism and gesticulation. The detail in Gentileschi's *San Tiburzio* is admirable; the picture as a whole is not. The curious alloy in Caravaggio's genius (which seems inseparable from his personality) was taken over with all its impurity, its baser metal (but without his genius), by his imitators. Latour did not deliberately extract its gold, purging away the dross; yet it was his art, however unsure of itself to

GENTILESCHI.   SAN TIBURZIO (DETAIL)

start with, that "filtered" Caravaggio's forms — it was not a rationalization of the latter's art.   In the *Magdalen with the Lamp* we have the exact colour of some of Caravaggio's pictures, that, for instance, of the Borghese *St John ;* yet the *Magdalen* is all "Latour" and is quite unlike the *St John.*   That line of the woman's profile in *The Cheat,* of the woman's profile in *The Prisoner* and that of the various *Magdalens* — now tracing a sweeping, all-embracing curve, and now broad, blunted angles — whose only precedent was the Florentine arabesque (very different, however, not because it has a narrower range, but because it outlines forms), that line which Caravaggio loathed, as Courbet would have loathed it, that line which permits of both the ripples in the Louvre *St Jerome* and the static trails of smoke in the *Adoration,* follows its imperious course, annexing and transforming what it can annex, destroying all the rest.   It draws nourishment from what, though seemingly quite alien, is intimately of its kind ; as a tree, from the leaf-mould at its roots.

Though of all great painters Caravaggio is the least coherent, his work has nevertheless a coherency that hinders its being "anatomized" whether by skill or even

CARAVAGGIO.   THE DEATH OF THE VIRGIN (FRAGMENT)

genius. Latour seems to have been captivated by what was purest in Caravaggio's art,
but he took over only its themes (which he could easily have dispensed with) and certain
colour combinations, which he proceeded to transform. He began by isolating a cycle
of it, which indeed holds our interest chiefly thanks to him, for Caravaggio's black-
and-red compositions are far from showing him at his splendid best.

What the "symbolic" Latour into whom three centuries have crystallized the
living artist must have most admired in Caravaggio was surely his boldly and broadly

rendered figures : the weeping woman in the foreground of *The Death of the Virgin*, and certain faces such as that of Mary in this picture, or the Augsburg *Lute-Player*. He equalled them ; what did he take over from them ? Precisely nothing.

Latour's "secret" is that which differentiates the women in *St Sebastian* from those in *The Death of the Virgin*.

Like some other processes of creative art, this would have been better understood had it not encountered a deeply rooted but erroneous belief : that genius is capable of

CARAVAGGIO.   THE DEATH OF THE VIRGIN (DETAIL)

GEORGES DE LATOUR.   ST SEBASTIAN BEWAILED BY ST IRENE (DETAIL)

improving on what has gone before. The theory that there exists an absolute, ideal perfection, and that it is for genius to attain this, is quite other than the notion of the rectification by genius of an inharmonious art; yet the two notions tend to overlap. A survey of the past, glimpsing beyond the ornate civilization of Versailles the stately harmony which, for their glory, Michelangelo bestowed on Florence and the Capitol, fosters the illusion that sees in every form of classicism either a primitivism made harmonious or a Baroque brought to heel. But is Velázquez a Titian or a Ribera made harmonious or controlled? What sort of Baroque is "brought to heel" in the Nouans *Pietà*.

We had better name "tradition" the nostalgic yearning for that serene and spacious art which reappears in several styles — not necessarily midway in their respective courses: in Van Eyck's *Adam,* for example — and gives an immediate impression of the artist's complete mastery of his medium. But whereas the pseudo-classic (like the English Pre-Raphaelites) pins his faith to a continuity of forms, the true classic sponsors a continuity of conquest. A conquest of forms which *afterwards* are found to be perpetuating a tradition. There is, no doubt, a genius of continuity; but it works through metamorphoses, and any notion of "improving on" anything is quite alien to it. Raphael is not an improved Perugino; he is Raphael. As for the other sort of tradition, it does not admit of rationalization; it was not Titian's whole-hearted disciples who carried on the torch, nor yet those who like the Carracci tried to modify him; it was Tintoretto, Rubens and Velázquez.

Thus Latour did not assign Caravaggio a place in an unbroken lineage; he created a plastic world of his own — without borrowing a single element of that world from Caravaggio, to whom, indeed, it was quite unknown. True, he took over his colours, forms and light — as he took colours, forms and a certain light from reality; and none the less transformed them. Never has a master vied with a previous master by judiciously modifying his art, or by imposing a thought-out stylization. "The thing is to combine the movement and shadows of the Venetians with Raphael's drawing": thus the Carracci. To render the movement of Venetian figures by some other kind of drawing? But their movement is implicit in their calligraphy; as a glance at a Carracci demonstrates. In the last analysis what this "improving on" or "perfecting" means is the rectification sponsored by the anthologist, but he operates only through suppressions. He makes cuts in *Booz endormi,* but he did not begin by writing it. The life of genius is an organic growth like that of a plant or a human body.

Thus Caravaggio's art, which was all realism, dramatic effect and sumptuous splendour (also, perhaps, an arraignment of the world) becomes, in Latour's hands, a far more delicate art, pensive and crystalline, which weaves a limpid music, reconciling man with God. Nowhere do we see more clearly the metamorphosis which, like a blood-stream, pulses throughout the history of art. Latour uses what he takes from Caravaggio as Christian architects used the stones of pagan Rome : to build churches "for the greater glory of God."

The same path led Poussin to become the Poussin we know, with this difference that his proximate masters were inferior to Caravaggio and those he chose for himself greater. And that he believed in "an art of all time" wherein he wished to carve out for himself a place. Overruling the styles of illusionist realism, he set out to recapture *style*, and to replace pleasure of the senses by what he named "delectation." He perceived that Raphael gave the art of Antiquity a new lease of life not with his Roman profiles, but with the least "antique" elements in his *School of Athens*. And he searched for the equivalent in painting of the antique line ; but, starting from bas-relief, he ended up with landscape. He began, like Latour, by demolishing the style of plastic realism by the usage of flat planes and "abstract" passages, which regulate the rest of the

POUSSIN. CRUCIFIXION

picture (and which cleaning brings out more clearly since the varnish and the sanguine ground on which he painted and which now "comes up" had tended to make his colours blend) — those flat planes to which, from Piero della Francesca onwards, heirs of the "grand style" are ever apt to have recourse. Such of his pictures as have been cleaned — especially the *Bacchanalia* in the London National Gallery — show how modern this art which aspired to be traditionalist, can look, and why there once was talk of his "astounding brio." Our cautious French cleaning, which revives above all the highlights, reveals on his misted canvases that which likens him to Corot rather than what he has in common with Cézanne. But if we wish to see how far his art actually is from those decorative Louis XIV mannerisms which mask it rather than express it, we have only to confront with works of the Bologna school or the later Venetians his *Bacchanalia*, the *Massacre of the Innocents*, the women on the right in *Eliezer and Rebecca* (who belong to the picture Louis XIV got from Richelieu) and, especially, the rediscovered *Crucifixion*, and the celestial steeds in *L'Empire de Flore*.

This "conquest" would have taken the same course had he belonged to the other race. Botticelli, to all appearances, took after Filippo Lippi, no less than Latour after Caravaggio. To begin with, both did homage to the prevailing taste of the period, as powerful then in Florence as was to be a century later in Venice that community of

taste we see in all the great Venetians. A taste deriving from the art of the miniature-painters and gold-workers, it deployed ringlets in cunning arabesques, spangled Minerva's robe with flowers, and bathed centaurs, cherubs and trees in the mellow light of a late-summer afternoon. (It was this which led Leonardo to say of Botticelli that "he did not know the first thing about landscape.") And Lippi did more than any other to impose this taste on Florence. This alliance of Christianity with mythology and the technique of the goldsmith was, after four and a half centuries, to modify women's *coiffures* once more and, for many years, its calligraphy was common to all Florentine masters — but as their *lowest* common measure. As for what was more vital in their art, we need only compare some of Botticelli's and Lippi's later works, to see how the former metamorphosed his teacher. This would have been done long ago, were it not that

so many of Lippi's works were painted in collaboration with Fra Diamante, and Botticelli's are often of small dimensions.

Lippi was primarily an ornate Masaccio. Lacking his greatness and intent on charm — the famous Florentine "grace" and that other, frailer and perhaps more Gothic (Italian Gothic is the Gothic of the ivory-carvers), which we associate with Baldovinetti. He painted a flounced and furbelowed Salome, while in his *St John Preaching* and *Nativity* he leaves alone the emphatic lines on which his talent saved him from embroidering and which his fondness for the decorative prevents from being modern. He is a refined colourist, who takes not a little pride in

FILIPPO LIPPI. NATIVITY OF ST STEPHEN (DETAIL)

his refinement. The horizontal mouldings on the wall in *Herod's Feast* are pink because Salome's dress is salmon-pink; this hue is repeated in the tiled floor, and it is this that gives their values to the yellows of the serving-maids and the violet of the figure with the clasped hands. That salmon-pink recurs in many of his works. Lippi's colour would often pass as "abstract" were it not put to the service of a glamour so familiar to us, that of Siena. Indeed sometimes we seem to see in him the painter through whom Siena, moribund in a lore of legends, makes her escape towards the glory that was — Florence . . .

Botticelli stood to Florentine taste as Tintoretto to Venetian taste; he liked it, made no effort to fight it, yet escaped from it as did Tintoretto from Venetian taste — one reason being that art ever eludes the nets of "taste." The misconception regarding him would not have become so firmly rooted, had not the earlier, lesser Botticelli owed so much to Lippi's *Madonna* of the Uffizi, had the Pre-Raphaelite movement never been, and, above all, were the dimensions of the last Botticellis those of the *Primavera*. It would then be plain to see that in the multiple scenes (for in these his composition consists of several compositions) of the London *Nativity* or *The Miracle of St Zenobius,* there is nothing left of Lippi, and we have here a painter very different from him whom Ruskin admired, and one who is still awaiting his posterity. A painter who "distorts" almost as much as El Greco, and whom his disregard of depth differentiates utterly from any Baroque artist. The torsion he gave his

FILIPPO LIPPI.   THE MADONNA OF THE UFFIZI

BOTTICELLI. NATIVITY (DETAIL)

line — no longer implementing the decorative, and serving no representational end save its own expression — led up (coupled with his predilection for airborne figures) to this *Nativity*. There are good reasons for studying piecemeal the details of this panel: not only do they throw light on the angels in *The Birth of Venus* and the woman quaintly nibbling a twig in *Primavera*, but they also show that Botticelli's treatment of nude figures — his Venus, his "Truth" in *The Calumny of Apelles* — runs counter to the common conceptions of his art. It is no mere chance that Northern painters have been so much impressed by them; knots of fine-spun lines enwrap their shining smoothness, much as the knotted muscles ripple on some of Michelangelo's seemingly unfinished figures. Lippi, the monk, slept with his nun without a qualm; whereas Botticelli burnt his early pictures (we must not forget how many of his "pagan" works perished in the flames). Far more than the famous "Remorse" in *The Calumny,* the kiss given Christ, the Virgin and the near-by figure in the Munich *Pietà* are not only symbols of the last phase of Botticelli's art, but also have much to tell us of his earlier phase; perhaps the Florence

FILIPPO LIPPI.   NATIVITY (FRAGMENT)

awaiting Savonarola, no less than that later Florence vainly trying to forget him, took thought for something more than garlands of gay flowers.

Why seek farther afield, when there is an example on a vaster scale : the metamorphosis of Byzantine into Romanesque art ? Romanesque art is neither more nor less closely linked to its forerunner than Latour to Caravaggio, or Botticelli to Lippi. True, the Vézelay tympanum was inspired by a miniature ; yet, once that origin established, we are interested no longer in learning in what respect the tympanum is like the miniature, but in what respects it departs from it : what its creator has made of it. Insects' tools are their limbs, with which they are equipped from birth and which they cannot change ; but genius puts forth unseen hands which, throughout the artist's working life, are ever changing, and enable him to derive from forms, those of the living and those whose lot it is to outlive death, the makings, often unforeseeable, of his metamorphosis. How strange that this far-flung world of ours, so fleeting yet eternal, should, if it is not to repeat but to renew itself, have such compelling need of Man !

BIBLIOGRAPHICAL NOTE

Some extracts from *The Twilight of the Absolute,* of which this is the first edition, were published in *Liberté de l'esprit* and *World Review* (London).

Also, some quotations from it were made in lectures delivered by the author in the course of 1949.

INDEX

Note : The index employs standard spellings. Variant spellings appear occasionally in the text. Italic figures indicate illustrations.

E

I

J

THE TWILIGHT OF THE ABSOLUTE,
THIRD VOLUME OF
THE PSYCHOLOGY OF ART
BY ANDRÉ MALRAUX,
WAS PRINTED BY L'IMPRIMERIE LA CONCORDE,
LAUSANNE, SWITZERLAND
FINISHED THE THIRTIETH DAY OF NOVEMBER
NINETEEN HUNDRED AND FIFTY
PRINTED IN SWITZERLAND